CARS of the 1950s

BY THE AUTO EDITORS OF CONSUMER GUIDE®

Publications International, Ltd.

Credits

Photography:

The editors would like to thank the following people and organizations for supplying the photography that made this book possible. They are listed below, along with the page number(s) of their photos.

Robert J. Anderson: 13; Scott Baxter: 125; Ken Beebe: 116; John Blake: 153; Rob Burrington: 11, 15; Chan Bush: 10, 17, 29, 69; Craig Caugh: 156; John Conde: 9, 11, 127, 148; Tony Eboli: 22; Randy Edmonds: 19; Jim Frenak: 34, 145; Mitch Frumkin: 59; Nina Fuller: 55; Thomas Glatch: 13, 18, 28, 29, 43, 48, 55, 57, 82, 118, 121, 146, 155; David Gooley: 9; Gary Greene: 33, 51, 104, 116, 121; Sam Griffith: 9, 70, 75, 85, 86, 90, 96, 97, 103, 104, 115, 116, 120, 130, 132, 170, 171, 173, 180; Jerry Heasley: 117; Don Heiny: 32, 34, 36, 47, 56, 91, 99, 109, 138; S. Scott Hutchinson: 123; David Jensen: 61; Bud Juneau: 12, 33, 39, 51, 53, 62, 67, 70, 105, 110, 118, 119, 126, 131, 143, 157, 160, 182; D. J. Kava: 12; Laurel Kenney, Jr.: 73; Tim Kerwin: 23; Milton Gene Kieft: 21, 26, 30, 35, 42, 49, 53, 77, 87, 119, 137, 139, 147, 150, 157; Lloyd Koening: 72; Rick Lenz: 147; Ed Lobit: 153, 158; Dan Lyons: 52, 104, 126, 133, 147, 151, 152, 160, 163; Vince Manocchi: 9, 10, 12, 31, 39, 42, 43, 45, 46, 47, 49, 50, 54, 55, 57, 58, 59, 61, 64, 65, 68, 69, 75, 78, 79, 81, 83, 84, 88, 92, 95, 99, 100, 104, 105, 106, 108, 109, 110, 113, 115, 117, 118, 119, 120, 122, 123, 124, 125, 128, 129, 131, 132, 133, 135, 137, 138, 139, 140, 141, 142, 145, 148, 149, 153, 154, 161, 162, 164, 166, 172, 176, 177, 180, 186; Doug Mitchel: 12, 30, 35, 43, 46, 53, 62, 63, 64, 66, 78, 80, 83, 89, 94, 95, 100, 106, 108, 109, 112, 113, 114, 115, 121, 122, 124, 127, 128, 134, 152, 165, 169, 175, 184, 192; Ron Moorhead: 104; Mike Mueller: 40, 49, 62, 68, 79, 84, 89, 114, 123, 125, 127, 149, 158, 173; David Newhardt: 58, 103, 174; Neil Nissing: 179; Nina Padgett-Russin: 64, 103, 107, 141, 155, 182; David Patrayas: 78; Greg Price: 130; Rob Reaser: 110; Larry and Alice Richter: 46; D. Randy Riggs: 176; Jeff Rose: 29, 38; Dennis Rozanski: 69; Bill Schintz Studio: 41; Tom Shaw: 44, 121; Rick Simmons: 189; Gary Smith: 47, 51, 56, 95, 148; Mike Spenner: 132; Richard Spiegelman: 97, 190; Steve Statham: 73; Tom Storm: 63, 138; David Suter: 50; David Temple: 32, 34, 37, 45, 88, 91, 106; Marvin Terrell: 43; Gregory Thomas: 15; Phil Toy: 51, 56, 60, 63, 64, 90, 101, 105, 123, 129, 178, 179, 186, 188; Dan Vecchio: 41; W. C. Waymack: 9, 17, 20, 32, 35, 37, 46, 48, 56, 67, 75, 76, 80, 92, 94, 98, 99, 103, 104, 106, 107, 111, 117, 124, 126, 131, 133, 138, 139, 148, 165, 168; Joseph Wherry: 23; White Eagle Studio: 191; Hub Willson: 129, 146; Nicky Wright: 14, 19, 20, 27, 52, 54, 55, 57, 58, 59, 60, 80, 85, 90, 98, 101, 107, 113, 114, 115, 120, 124, 125, 129, 133, 135, 136, 150, 161, 163, 167, 174, 181, 183, 184, 185, 187, 189, 190; Vince Wright: 79, 134

Front Cover: Ron Kimball Photography
Back Cover: Bud Juneau; Vince Manocchi; Doug Mitchel; Phil Toy

Owners:

Special thanks to the owners of the cars featured in this book for their cooperation.

Burt Carlson: 19; Paul Oxley: 52; George Buchinger: 147; Jerry Johnson: 148; Kenneth Lindsey: 149; Ken Netwig: 152; John Boyle: 125; Richard Beggs and Maureen McCullough: 116; Verne Leyendecker/Classical Gas: 153; Terry Gale: 11, 15; Bob and Wendi Walker: 10; Robert Walker: 17; T. L. Ary: 29; Bob Reed: 69; Ervin Irish: 156; John Oakes, Jr.: 22; Michael Stecco: 19; Joseph A. Herzberg: 34; Jack Miller: 145; Jim Crossen: 59; Neil Martin/Goldenrod Garage: 55; Albie Albershardt: 13; Ted Hinkle: 28; Len Antrim: 29; David L. Studer: 43; Bob Strous and Lizzie Pusch: 48; Tom Devers: 55; Ron and Donna Krauss: 57; Tom Griffith: 82; Robert Bymers: 118; Henry Koenig: 121; Ken Griesemer: 146; Jim Morschack: 155; Kathy Crasweller: 9; Gordon Apker: 33, 51; Howard Von Pressentin: 104; James Emmi: 116; Ken and Esther Thompson: 121; Chicago Car Exchange: 9, 112, 169, 180; Earl Heintz: 70; Glen Gangestad: 75; Jerry Capizzi/Cappy Collection™: 85, 96, 97; Stephan Thomas: 86; Robb Petty: 90; Bobby Wiggins: 103; Mike and Nancy McCutcheon: 104; William and Joseph Schoenbeck: 115; Carl Herren: 116; Ray and Myrna Boznarth: 120; John Petras: 121, 130, 132; Richard Presson: 170, 171; Gary Thompson: 173; Billie Markos: 117; Charles W. Park: 32; Ernest C. Fodor: 32; Chip Loree: 34; Fred Katen: 36; Michael W. Riebe: 47; James Rudolph: 56; Thomas Amendola, Sr.: 79, 91; Bob Schlenk: 99; Ray Riddick: 109; Joe Carfagna: 138; James Cunningham: 123; Christopher Antal: 61; Dennis Flint: 12; Norman Frey: 33; Tim L. Graves: 39; Bill Stone: 51; Ralph M. Hartsock: 53; Dennis B. Miracky: 62; Jerry and Jackie Lew: 67; Jack Karleskind: 70, back cover; Dug and Sonja Waggoner: 105; Bob Heffman: 110; Mac Horst: 118; Joe Malta: 119; Robert Matteoli and Charlene Arora: 126; Glyn-Jan Rowley: 131; Doug Burnell: 143; William Albright: 143; Gerald Newton: 157; Greg Pagano: 116; Robert Sexton: 182; Charles Sharpe: 73; Dr. William Lenharth: 23; Bob Aaron: 21; Frank Wrenick: 26; Bob Porter: 30; Jeff Walther/Jeff Walther Dodge: 35; James and John Sharp: 42; Richard Brinker: 49; David Greibling: 53; William Lindsey: 77; Ross Gibaldi: 87; Edwin Kirstatter: 87; Kennedth and Wayne Turner: 119; Christine and Robert Waldock: 137; John Messmore: 137; Al Schaefer: 139; Rosemary and Duane Sell: 147; Clarence Becker: 150; Bill Wilt: 157; Henry Patrick: 72; Neil Greener: 147; Larry Landis: 153, 158; Jim Clark: 52;

Gary Kistinger: 104; Edward Ballenger, II: 126; Stephen Capone: 133; Steve Carey: 147; Deer Park Car Museum: 151; Robert Jones: 152; George Jewell: 160; Richard Lesson: 163; Samuel G. Tribble: 9; Wendy Walker: 10; Bill Lauer: 10, 64; Thomas Null: 12; Rudy and Carolyn Hester: 31; Richard L. Leu: 31; Art Astor: 39, 99; David Cutler: 42; Jack Pinsker: 42; Gerry Capp: 43; William H. Lauer and Robert L. McAtee: 45; Harry DeMenge: 46, 47; Aivar Lejins: 54, 58, 59, 64; Charles Phoenix: 55; Bill Hughes: 55; Sherwood Kahlenberg: 57; Aaron Kahlenberg: 61; Richard Carpenter/Yesterday Once More: 49, 65; John Roger: 68; Nancy Beauregard: 69; Tom Howard: 75; Alan and Elaine Franklin: 78; Jerry James: 79; Ray Scherr: 81; Tony Smith: 83; Sandra Simpkin: 84; Lynn Augustine: 88; Bob Rose: 92; Tom Turner: 95; Neil Schwartz: 99; William Kipp: 100; Dave Higby: 104; Morgan Woodward: 105; Donald Baldwin: 106; John Murray: 108; Richard Clements: 108; Bernie Hackett: 108; John Milliken: 109; Roy and Bonnie McClain: 110; Chuck and Laurie Abbott: 113; Ray Ostrander: 115; David Ferguson: 115; Richard and Janice Plastino: 117; Steve Rostam: 118; Greg Gustafson: 119; On and Barbara Gerger: 120; Bill and Margaret Hunter: 122; Robert Supalla: 123; Orville Dopps: 123; Richard Hibbard: 124; Burke Chaplin: 125; Mark Johnson Trust: 128; Richard Zeiger, MD: 128; Bob Vice: 129; Dick Hoigt: 131; Kris Trexler: 132, 139; Jerry Hammer: 132; Gerald Depersio: 132; Michael Porto: 50, 132; Jim Blanchard: 133; Jerry Cinotti: 135; Phil Trost: 137; Robert and Diane Adams: 138; Beau Day: 140; Jim Davidson: 141; Garth Higgins: 141; Dix Helland: 142; Wayne Graefen: 145, back cover; John Parker: 148; Tom Null: 149; Pete Dunkel: 153; Dann Whalen: 154; Mark and Jan Hilbert: 161; Keith Bartlett: 164; Paul and Chris Baldassarre: 166; Richard Marks: 166; Art and Jared Rosen: 172, 176; Joseph Bua: 177, back cover; Russell McCauley: 180; Paul and Donna Parla: 186; Vern Burkitt: 12; Robert Schnoes: 12; Thomas Milfort: 30, 113; Walter F. Thomas: 35; Donald Merz: 43; Ron Yori: 46; Richard E. Bilter: 53; Guy Morice: 62; Galen and Fay Erb: 63; Tom Green: 64; Ken Bounds: 66; George Lucie: 78; Gary Blakeslee: 80, back cover; Dennis Hardison: 83; Gerry Klein: 89; Jerry Robbin: 94; Bill and Collette Stanley: 94; William Mucci: 95; Phil Schaefer: 100; Steve Bergin: 106; Chester Pallach: 108; Rick Holmes: 109; Gary Morrison: 112; Hank Roeters: 112; Art Lostumo, Jr.: 114; Dave Comstock: 115; Bruce Dockery: 124; Jim Ferrero: 127; Bill and Anna Harper: 127; Joe Bortz: 128; Frank Bobek: 128; John Strewe: 134; Jeff Griffith: 152; Dick Moore: 165; Jim Ingersoll: 175; Herbert Wehling: 184; Alan Wendland: 192; Roy Asbahr: 104; Stanley and Phyllis Dumes: 40; Jim Scarpitti: 49; A. LaRue Plotts, Jr.: 49; Bob and Roni Sue Shapiro: 62; Jim Mueller: 68, 84, 122; Eugene Vaughn: 79; Priceless Classic Motorcars: 89; John Galandak: 114; John Cavanaugh: 123; Edward Kuziel: 125; David and Anne Kurtz: 127; David Horton: 149; Joseph Ezell: 158; Robert Hetzel: 173; Paul Schinnerer: 58; James Greene: 103; Ron Wakefield: 174; Jerry Kill: 179; Roger Irland: 64; Wally Herman: 103; Bob and Gail Elwood: 107; Tom Edmier: 141; Richard Belveal: 155; Ken Mooney: 182; David Horn: 78; Duane and Steven Stupienski: 130; Gary Bacon: 110; Dorsey Lewis: 46; James Schoffstall: 189; Jim Wickel: 176; Frank and Elaine Wrenick: 29; Butch's Rod Shop: 38; Frederick Schillinger: 69; Mearl Zeigler: 41; Darrell and Jaqué Davis: 44; Charles Jackson: 121; Wayne Simonson: 47; Bob Riggs: 56; Don and Carol Berg: 95; Mike and Karen Barker: 148; Frank Lyle: 12; Anthony Robert Herk, Jr.: 97; Dave Frieday: 190; Robert C. Donatucci: 63; William Smith: 138; Douglas Dressler: 50; Michael Pittmon: 32; Joop Van Egmond: 34; Motor Cars Ltd.: 37; Dick Nelson: 45; Royce and Clydette Kidd: 45; Z.T. Parker: 88; Jim Hollingsworth: 91; Austin Kelley: 106; Bob and Roni Sue Shapiro: 43; Jay and Jamie Lou Wheaton: 15; Brockers Beautys: 51; Frank Pfaffinger: 56; Ole S. Jensen: 60; Brent Walker: 63, 90, back cover; Richard Palmer: 64; Carl and Mary Allen: 73; Sal Orlando: 101; Bob Garcia: 105; Kit Lee: 123; Cars of San Francisco, Inc.: 129, back cover; Ron Hagen: 178; George Ferrick: 179; Tom Shafer, Steve and Kathleen Clarke: 186; Jeff Wade: 188; R. Clark Goodwin, DDS: 41; Steve Blake: 9; Bill Hubert: 17; Larry Martin: 17, 35, 56, 76, 99; Clifford Elmore: 20; Arvel and Barbara Froemling: 32; Ardie and Doris Sabo: 32; Tom Taylor: 35; Robert S. Kerico: 37; David H. Cramer: 46; Glen Weeks: 48; Wilbert Sackman: 67; Andrew Surmeier: 75, 103; Jan and Mike Thomas: 80; Eddie Bockholdt: 92; Milt Mouser: 94; Glen and Janice Pykiet: 94; Hank Degman: 94; Don and Wanda Spivey: 98; Gary Marshall: 104; John Clark: 106; Montey Carpenter: 107; Mary and Marshall Simpkin: 111; Wayne and Pat Lasley: 111; Robert Sax: 117; Barbara Ann: 124; Roger Kinder: 126; Dale Mueth: 131; Homer Altevogt: 133; Bill Schwelitz: 138; Howard Funck: 139; Gene Marburger: 141; Gene Keepes: 165; Jerry and Barb Guthrie: 168; Edward Singleterry: 23; Paul Kirst: 191; Bill Ulrich: 129; Philomena Ronco Kohan: 146; Glendon and Betty Kierstead: 19; Harry Downing: 20; Douglas Suter: 27; Glen and Barbara Patch: 52; Jess Ruffalo: 54, 59, 60; Glen Patch: 57, 183; Dean Ullmauck: 58; Fred and Diane Ives: 80; John Wood: 85; Richard Nassar: 90; Dennis Huff: 98; Steve and Dawn Cizmas: 101; Jerry Ferguson: 107; Dick Choler: 113; Blaine Jenkins: 114; Ed Oberhaus: 115; Bob Flack: 120; Sherry Echols: 124; Wayne Rife: 129; Marvin Wallace: 133; Barry and Barbara Bales: 135; Jim DiGregorio: 55, 135; Walter Smith: 136; Don Kreider: 136; Richard Matson: 14, 150; Edward Ostrowski: 161; Dr. Douglas Bruinsma: 163; Steve Megyesi: 167; Patrick Billey: 174; Don Waite: 181; Tim and Sharon Hacker: 183; Donald Lawson: 184; Studebaker National Museum, Inc.: 185; Thomas Karkiewicz: 187; Andrew Krizman: 189; Don and Bonnie Sniper: 190; Mark Apel: 134

Special thanks to the photographic and media services groups of the following organizations:

California Department of Transportation; Daimler-Chrysler, Ford Motor Company; General Motors Corporation; United Press Photo

CONTENTS

FOREWORD   6

AMERICAN MOTORS CORPORATION   8
Hudson, Metropolitan, Nash, Rambler

CHRYSLER CORPORATION   30
Chrysler, DeSoto, Dodge, Imperial, Plymouth

FORD MOTOR COMPANY   66
Continental, Edsel, Ford, Lincoln, Mercury

GENERAL MOTORS CORPORATION   102
Buick, Cadillac, Chevrolet, Oldsmobile, Pontiac

HUDSON   142

KAISER-FRAZER CORPORATION   146
Frazer, Kaiser, Willys

NASH   150

PACKARD   158

STUDEBAKER   164

STUDEBAKER-PACKARD CORPORATION   172

FOREWORD

A retrospective look at the Fifties reveals a decade of enthusiasm and optimism, underscored by a touch of innocence. But it was also a time of great change. Television overtook radio as the foremost influence on popular culture, which also gradually embraced the rebellious overtones of a new sound called rock 'n' roll.

Yet nowhere was change more evident than in the automobiles advertised on those flickering TV screens. Each year brought a new twist on "longer, lower, wider," along with ever-taller tailfins and ever-more chrome. And let us not forget the horsepower race, which prompted many manufacturers to *triple* power output during the 10-year period.

Relived in countless movies, books, and TV sit-coms over the years, the Fifties hold an attraction to generations not yet born during its time. And the excitement of this fascinating era was duly reflected in the cars Americans bought—and still enjoy today.

It was a financial shotgun wedding that brought longtime manufacturers Hudson and Nash together in 1954 to form American Motors Corporation.

Hudson was the older of the two marques, having been established in 1909, nearly a decade before the first Nash appeared. Hudson had long been a midprice make with an accent on performance, a reputation that blossomed during the early Fifties with the potent Hornet.

Nash was likewise a midprice make, but was known more for its stout construction, practicality, and operating economy. In the early Forties, Nash was one of the first companies to introduce true unitized construction, and set itself apart in the late Forties with its sleek "bathtub" styling.

After the postwar seller's boom subsided in the early 1950s, both companies found themselves being squeezed by the full-court sales press being applied by the Big Three—Ford Motor Co., General Motors, and Chrysler Corporation. Both Nash and Hudson turned to compacts as a means to provide choices the Big Three didn't. Nash had the Rambler, which was quite successful; Hudson had the Jet, which was not.

At the time of the merger, Nash was the stronger of the two, with twice as many sales. Much of this was due to the success of the compact Rambler, which would soon carry a Hudson badge as well, replacing the Jet in showrooms. Another shared model was the Metropolitan, a tiny two-seater Nash had begun importing from England in 1954.

Also shared by the two companies were 1955's redesigned mid- and full-size bodies, with each make boasting different nose and tail treatments. This probably saved money, but made each marque a little less special in the bargain. Sales soon tumbled for all but the Rambler and Metropolitan, which both became separate makes for 1957—just as the Hudson and Nash nameplates were sinking into the horizon. The two grand old marques disappeared after that, their compact progenies being left to march alone into the Sixties.

1

2

3

4

Opposite page: Top executives of the newly formed American Motors Corporation were (from left to right) Abraham E. Barit of Hudson, George W. Mason of Nash, and fellow Nash exec George Romney. Mason was named president of AMC, soon to be succeeded by Romney. *This page:* **1.** Hudson's Hornet was powered by a potent 308-cubic-inch flathead six that helped make it a stock-car-racing hero. Also contributing was its Step-down design, which placed the body between the Monobilt frame rails, thus lowering the center of gravity for better handling. **2.** As indicated by its trunklid badge, this 1954 Hornet club coupe is powered by Hudson's hot Twin H-Power six with twin carburetors and a mighty 170 horsepower. A special 7-X racing version reportedly put out close to 220 hp. Hudson's lower-priced Wasp looked like the Hornet, but was shorter and carried a smaller engine. **3.** A Hornet Brougham convertible topped the regular Hudson line at $3288. **4.** Hornet's big four-door sedan carried a long, sloping roofline and a $2769 price tag. **5.** At the opposite end of the 1954 spectrum was the compact Jet, with a 202-cid six. A flashy $2057 Jet Liner sedan is shown, but other models started as low as $1621. **6.** Built in Italy with an aluminum body atop a Jet chassis, the exotic Hudson Italia cost an equally exotic $4800—and sold just 26 copies.

5

6

1. If Hudson was known as a racetrack demon, Nash was known as a mobile motel. This ad mentions the fact that a Nash's seats could be folded down to form a bed. But by 1954, nearly everyone already knew it. No father ever wanted to see his daughter's date arrive in a Nash. **2.** The company's top 1954 sedan was the $2600 Ambassador Custom. Power for the big Ambassadors came from a 252-cubic-inch six with 140 horsepower. A midprice line, the Statesman, shared the Ambassador's styling, but was shorter in length and powered by a smaller 100-hp six. **3.** With no convertible in the line, the $2735 Ambassador Custom Country Club coupe was the most expensive "regular" '54 Nash. With Nash's conservative image, it's no wonder it was outsold by its sedan counterpart by a 16-to-1 margin. **4.** Nash had its own exotic in the Italian-designed, British-built Nash-Healey. A convertible version was dropped for 1954, leaving a $6000 coupe that sold fewer than 100 copies before being discontinued itself.

1954 Nash Ambassador Custom Four-Door Sedan, photographed in scenic Ariz

1

2

3

4

1

2

3

1-2. A new addition to the Nash family was the baby Metropolitan. Imported from England, it carried a 74-cubic-inch four-cylinder engine boasting 42 horsepower—and great fuel economy. The coupe version cost $1445, the convertible just $1469.
3-4. The most popular boat in Nash's fleet was the compact Rambler, sales of which probably kept the company afloat during these years. A surprising number of body styles were offered: two- and four-door sedans and wagons, along with a two-door hardtop and a unique semiconvertible, actually a two-door sedan with a full fold-back fabric roof. Standard engine was a 185-cid 85-hp six, though a 90-hp six was also offered. Prices ranged from $1550 to $2050.

4

SCORECARD		1954
MAKE	TOTAL PRODUCTION	RANK
HUDSON	50,670 ▾	14th ▴
NASH	91,121 ▾	11th ▴

1

1. Hudson originally planned to introduce a mere update to the Step-down design for 1955, but the merger with Nash brought an entirely different car.
2-3. And this was it. Bodyshells were shared with Nash, but aside from the reverse-slant rear roof pillar, it was hard to tell; both makes sported wildly different front and rear styling. Hudson arguably got the better end of the deal, yet its sales went down while Nash's went up. Shown are top-line Hornets in two-door-hardtop and four-door-sedan guise; there was no more convertible. With the standard 308-cubic-inch flathead six with 160/170 horsepower or the newly available 320-cid V-8 with 208, Hornet prices ranged from $2565 to $3145.
4-5. Wasps again looked similar, but rode a shorter wheelbase and came with a not-very-sporty 202-cid six with 110-120 hp. Shown is the $2460 Custom sedan. All Hudsons adopted Nash's famous Weather-Eye heating and ventilation system.
6. Hudson ads boasted that its full-sized offerings had the widest seats and most head room of *any* car—odd, since Nash's Ambassador had the same body.

2

3

4

5

6

1

2

1-2. Hudson dealers must have rejoiced when they got their first batch of popular Ramblers, despite the fact they differed from Nashes mainly in grille badging. It's doubtful competing Nash dealers were quite as enthused. Ramblers had an economy-minded 195-cubic-inch six with 90 horsepower and were priced as low as $1457, though Custom models like those shown cost close to two grand. **3.** A Hudson Statesman enters as a Hudson Rambler (a name that surely raised the ire of Nash dealers) leaves.

3

1. The redesigned 1955 Ambassador carried over Nash's traditional skirted fenders, and featured inboard headlights that gave it a unique "face." An Ambassador Country Club hardtop cost $3095 with the new 320-cubic-inch 208-horsepower V-8 that was shared with Hudson, or $2795 with a 252-cid 130-hp six that was not. 2. Nash's dashboard retained its center-focused styling theme, with the speedometer offset to the right of the steering wheel. This Statesman is equipped with air conditioning, an option to Nash's excellent Weather-Eye heating and ventilation system. 3. As before, the Statesman mirrored Ambassador styling, but on a shorter wheelbase.

2

3

1

2

1. Rambler's value equation was a strong selling point. Not only was the car inexpensive to buy and run, but resale value had been high as well. Prices started at $1585—about the same as a really stripped '55 Chevrolet—with air conditioning and automatic transmission optional. **2.** A Custom Cross Country wagon was the most expensive Rambler at $2098. **3-4.** Top-line Rambler sedans and coupes shared their big brother's reverse-slant rear roof pillar. Lower-level models had a traditional sloping roof pillar. Nash's Rambler outsold Hudson's version by more than nine-to-one, and outsold all other Nashes combined.

3

4

SCORECARD		1955
MAKE	TOTAL PRODUCTION	RANK
HUDSON	46,000 ▼	15th ▼
NASH	126,000 ▲	11th ●

IT'S HERE !.. THE BIG CAR WITH BIG CHANGES
THE NEW 1956 HUDSON HORNET WITH THE NEW V-8

Tune in "Disneyland" — ABC-TV Network

Hudson Hornet Hollywood Hardtop V-8

Alive with new V-8 power! Sleek with new V-Line styling! Luxurious with new, high-fashion, color-matched exteriors and interiors!

Here you see the mighty Hornet V-8 with even more power and performance for '56 than it's ever had through all the years it's held the National Performance Championship.

Here you see the great performer all dressed up with distinguished, new, high-fashion V-line styling inside and out that stamps it at once as the year's car of distinction.

Here's the car that sets you smartly apart from the crowd. Take your choice of V-8 or 6, of 15 new two-tone and 6 new three-tone color exteriors, with stunning new interiors color-keyed to match. Now, more than ever, the new 1956 Hornet V-8 is the most beautiful performer of them all. Be sure to see it for yourself at your Hudson dealer's now.

Sizzling getaway from zero to sixty in 12½ split seconds! That's the Hornet's great, new 220-hp. V-8 engine! Far advanced in short-stroke, low-friction, over-head-valve design, proved in millions of miles of rugged testing, you'll like its "lift," its eagerness to go!

Hudson Hornets • Wasps • Ramblers • Metropolitans

Built the Better Way — the American Way — Products of American Motors

New color-matched interiors and exteriors! Here's standout new styling with exciting new in-terior fabrics, color-matched with 21 new two- and three-tone exterior finishes of your choice. And the new V-Line styling is refreshingly different.

Three times softer, steadier ride! Hudson's new Deep Coil Ride gives you three times the cushioning comfort of most car springs. It's possible only with exclusive Double Safe Single Unit car construction.

OTHER CARS

HUDSON HORNET V-8
The most beautiful performer of them all!

1

16

2

3

4

1-5. Hudson was trying really hard—perhaps *too* hard—to keep up with the flashy new offerings from the Big Three. The 1956 Hornet added small fins to its front and rear fenders, could be ordered in 15 two-tone and six three-tone color combinations, and adopted a huge "smiling" grille. But it turned out there would be little to smile about, as for all this effort, sales of the big Hudsons (Hornet and Wasp) retreated to less than 11,000 units—about half the '55 total. Hornet's available V-8 first grew to 352 cubic inches and 220 horsepower, then was replaced by a 250-cid, 190-hp engine.

6. A redesigned Rambler boasted considerably altered styling, but it's hard to say it was an improvement. Whether wearing a Nash or Hudson badge, sales didn't come close to matching 1955's figures. Body styles were trimmed to include only four-doors: a sedan, a wagon, a hardtop sedan, and the nation's first hardtop wagon. Prices went up, now starting at $1829, but the sales decline may have been due more to its association with the names Hudson and Nash, which were sinking fast.

5

6

1

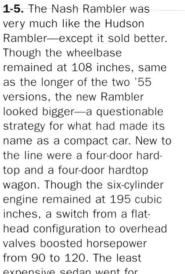

2

1-5. The Nash Rambler was very much like the Hudson Rambler—except it sold better. Though the wheelbase remained at 108 inches, same as the longer of the two '55 versions, the new Rambler looked bigger—a questionable strategy for what had made its name as a compact car. New to the line were a four-door hard-top and a four-door hardtop wagon. Though the six-cylinder engine remained at 195 cubic inches, a switch from a flat-head configuration to overhead valves boosted horsepower from 90 to 120. The least expensive sedan went for $1829, just $40 less than a comparable '56 Chevrolet. Sales score: Rambler, 10,000. Chevy, 1.5 million. Hmm.

Crowning The Greatest Success Of Any New Make In Nearly Two Decades

American Motors Presents THE ALL-NEW, ALL-AMERICAN **'56 Rambler**

4

The NEW CONCEPT in Station Wagon Travel

The All-New All-American **Rambler** CROSS COUNTRY STATION WAGON

5

3

1

2

3

1-3. Nash needed a stylish new design to bounce back from a rather dismal 1955. It didn't get it. But with sales so poor, it's surprising the company spent the money to do anything at all. Rear ends were taller and more squared off, front ends added vertical parking light pods at the forward edge of the fenders. 4. Once in their lives everyone should drive a '50s car, so that on a handling scale of 1 to 10, they'll know what a zero feels like. A '56 Nash will do nicely. 5. Late in the '56 model year, the tiny Metropolitan imported from England was updated with a slightly revised front end and a larger 90-cubic-inch, 52-horsepower engine.

4

5

SCORECARD		1956
MAKE	TOTAL PRODUCTION	RANK
HUDSON	35,671 ▼	15th ●
NASH	83,420 ▼	12th ▼

1

2

3

4

5

1-5. Nineteen fifty-seven would prove to be Hudson's last hurrah. The company greeted the model year with a mildly revised Hornet, now flying alone as the shorter Wasp departed the nest. Prices for the surviving V-8 models were lower, but entry-level prices were higher because the six-cylinder versions were history. Power came from a 327-cubic-inch V-8 rated at 255 horsepower—35 more than the top '56 engine. Styling changes were predictably minimal: taller tacked-on fins in back, *dual* tacked-on fins in front, and altered side trim. Total sales barely topped 4000 units, and, with that, the once proud Hudson nameplate bid the land adieu. It was a sad end for a company that just four years earlier had been the terror of the stock-car tracks.

1

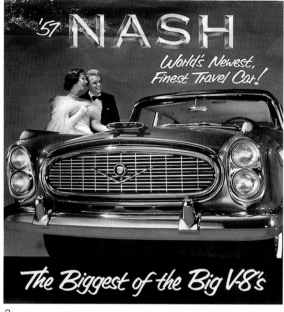

2

3

1-3. Nash made a valiant effort to stay afloat with a surprisingly effective facelift for '57. Where it was legal, it boasted dual headlights a year before most makes adopted them. Nashes shared the 327 V-8 found in surviving Hudsons and likewise were reduced to a single model. Ambassador prices started at $2586—$235 less than Hornet's—but model-year production was even lower, at 3600. AMC saw the writing on the wall, put the bleeding Nash nameplate out of its misery, and staked the corporate future on the compact Rambler. Never again would a new Nash fold its seats to afford its owners a free night's sleep.

1-3. AMC chose to distance the Rambler from its failing linemates by making it a separate make for 1957; note the "R" on the hubcaps. Sales skyrocketed, led by the $2500 six-cylinder Custom Cross Country station wagon. Three-tone color combinations were offered, along with Rambler's first V-8, the 250-cubic-inch 190-horsepower engine fitted to late-'56 Ambassadors and Hornets. **4-6.** But an even *bigger* V-8—the 327-cid engine used in the '57 Nashes and Hudsons—was stuffed into a Rambler to produce the hot-rod Rebel. Horsepower was raised from 255 to 270 for this application, and in the light, 3300-lb four-door hardtop, made for a "sleeper" road rocket that previewed the formula used by muscle cars of the next decade. Rebels were said to be quicker than every other '57 car but the Corvette. **7-8.** Also gaining its independence this year was the tiny English-built Metropolitan, which likewise got its own insignia on its hubcaps. And it likewise showed a big sales gain—from 7645 to 13,425—despite a slight price increase that set the coupe at $1567 and the convertible at $1591.

2

1

3

4

5

6

7

8

1

1. With Hudson and Nash relegated to history, AMC could focus its development dollars on the Rambler, which sprouted fins and got a facelift for 1958. Wheelbase remained at 108 inches and the basic body structure carried over, but the look was all new. The 195-cubic-inch six returned as the standard engine. A revised 250-cid V-8 gained 25 horsepower for a total of 215, and all models so equipped were called "Rebel V-8." Sadly, their namesake—the hot-rod '57 Rebel—was dropped. The attraction of Rambler's fuel economy is evident in the fact the vast majority sold were powered by the six-cylinder engine. **2.** Despite its compact pretensions, the Rambler was touted as a six-passenger vehicle. Although ads proclaimed they could be "six big 6-footers with their hats on," half a dozen folks who were small and very friendly would have been a more comfortable fit. Wagons drew the most advertising attention—and the most sales.

2

Presenting Rambler For 1958

RAMBLER ECONOMY 6

RAMBLER REBEL V-8

AND NOW . . . ALL-NEW
Ambassador V-8

Who Said A Fine Car Has To Be "Big As All Outdoors"?

Mr. J. E. Coleman of Alexandria, Ind., traded America's leading high-priced car for an Ambassador. Said Mr. Coleman: "I thought the car I was driving was big, but this year's models seemed even harder to park and get in my garage. After carefully looking the field over, I traded for an Ambassador. Has all the luxury features my former car offered plus easy parking and handling. Best of all, my Ambassador cost me a thousand dollars less than my former car."

Drive the 270 HP Ambassador V-8 . . . *the compact luxury car* on a 117-inch wheelbase. Easiest to park, fits any garage. Top power-to-weight ratio in its field . . . outstanding V-8 economy. Personalized Luxury: individually adjustable front seats. Lowest first cost—highest resale value of all medium-priced cars. At your Rambler dealer's.

Why struggle to park an overgrown 1959 car? Drive the one medium-priced car that slips easily into parking spaces other cars have to pass up. Ambassador out-handles and out-performs other medium-priced cars.

Other '59s too big for your garage? Unused room at downtown garages and lots? Most medium-priced cars are. But not Ambassador—the compact luxury car that fits any garage. See it at your Rambler dealer's.

finest car ever priced so close to the lowest **Ambassador** *by Rambler*

HOLIDAY/JUNE

2

1-2. Effectively replacing the departed Hudson and Nash in AMC's line was a new Ambassador. Borrowing the name of Nash's former top trim level, it was an upscale version of the Rambler built on a longer wheelbase. Power came from the 327-cubic-inch V-8 formerly used in the hot '57 Rebel.

1

1-2. The hardtop station wagon was unique to the Ambassador line and the most expensive model at $3116; other Ambassadors were priced about $250 upstream of comparable Rambler V-8s. Four Ambassador body styles accounted for 14,862 sales, double that of the final Hudson and Nash combined—which still isn't saying much.

1

2

1

2

3

1-2. In a fortuitous move, AMC president George Romney brought out a smaller Rambler just as the nation was falling into a recession. Christened the American, it wasn't actually new: He merely dusted off the dies last used to stamp out 1955 Nash Rambler coupes. The 100-inch-wheelbase American was offered only as a two-door, yet sold more than 30,000 copies in its inaugural year—and it would go up from there. Prices started at just $1775, no doubt an important element in its resounding success. Due to the recession, every major automaker saw a sales decline for 1958 except for Rambler—whose sales doubled. **3.** Still being offered was the tiny Metropolitan, with an 85-inch wheelbase and a starting price of $1626.

SCORECARD		1958
MAKE	TOTAL PRODUCTION	RANK
RAMBLER	186,227 ▲	7th ▲

1-2. Ambassador sales improved to more than 23,000 units for 1959, as the nation eased out of its recession. All had the 327-cubic-inch V-8 carried over from '58. A Custom four-door sedan cost $2732. **3.** Ambassador dashboards mimicked the design of lesser Ramblers, but were brushed with a bit more bright trim. **4.** Replacing a traditional automatic-transmission shift lever was a Telovac pushbutton control panel, which was mounted to the left side of the steering column. Similar to what Chrysler Corp. cars had used since 1956, Televac first appeared in '58, and continued as a Rambler feature into the Sixties.

1

3

2

4

1

2

3

1-2. A Rambler Custom six-cylinder sedan was a rather classy looking economy car—both inside and out. **3-4.** Added to the American line were two-door wagons, which, like the sedans, were merely resurrected from 1955. Only three of these enclosed sedan delivery versions were built. Interiors were decidedly stark next to those of upper-level Ramblers. American sales tripled in 1959, despite the fact that starting prices rose about $50 to $1821. Its success undoubtedly influenced the Big Three to come out with their own compact cars, which arrived en masse for 1960. **5.** Metropolitan sales were also up dramatically for '59, prices holding at $1626 for the coupe, $1650 for the jaunty convertible. The Rambler nameplate would continue through the 1960s, to be replaced by the AMC badge in the '70s. But falling sales and mounting losses prompted a takeover by Renault of France in 1982. The last true AMCs were built in 1987, and the corporate name was soon relegated to history.

4

5

SCORECARD		1959
MAKE	TOTAL PRODUCTION	RANK
RAMBLER	363,372 ▲	6th ▲

As the Fifties dawned, Chrysler Corporation cars were wearing the boxy, upright styling adopted in their 1949 redesign—styling that seemed rather dated even in its debut year. But corporate president K. T. Keller preferred a conservative look, in part a knee-jerk reaction to the failure of the corporation's radical Airflow streamliners of the 1930s.

Chrysler got its start in 1924 when founder Walter P. Chrysler acquired the ailing Maxwell/Chalmers company, soon rechristening it with his own name. The company's midpriced cars had hydraulic brakes well before most rivals, illustrating an emphasis on engineering that prevailed at Chrysler for decades to come. Dodge was acquired in 1928, followed by the introduction of the low-price Plymouth, midprice DeSoto, and upper-crust Imperial. This lineup resulted in a price "ladder," mimicking that which had made General Motors—for whom Walter P. Chrysler had formerly worked—such a success.

Chrysler's styling may have entered the Fifties like a lamb, but it went out like a lion. The pivotal year was 1955, when all of Chrysler Corporation's makes were restyled with thoroughly modern lines. They soon hosted among the largest and most radical fins of the era, with styling that took a back seat to no one. Equally noteworthy was the 1951 introduction of the famous hemi-head V-8. Soon known simply as the "Hemi," it would power stock-car victors, dragstrip winners, and ferocious street machines into the 1960s and beyond.

1

2

1. About as radical a Chrysler as could be found in the conservative 1950 lineup was the wood-trimmed Town & Country Newport hardtop coupe. Though prototype hardtops (without center roof pillars) were built a few years earlier, the 1950 models were the company's first production versions. This model's $4003 price topped even those of the luxury Imperials—by a lot. Only the low-production Crown Imperial limousines cost more. Upper-line Chryslers—Saratoga, New Yorker, Town & Country, and Imperial—rode a 131.5-inch wheelbase (Crown Imperial a 145.5-inch span)—and came with a 323-cubic-inch straight eight with 135 horsepower. **2.** By far the most popular 1950 Chrysler was this $2329 Windsor sedan. Comparable entry-level Royals cost a couple hundred dollars less. Windsor and Royal had a 125.5-inch wheelbase and a 250-cid six with 115 hp.

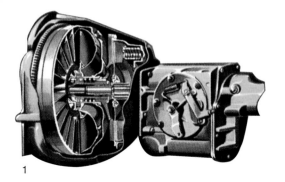

1

2

3

1. Lacking a true automatic transmission, Chrysler offered Fluid Drive starting in the early 1940s. Fluid Drive used a conventional manual transmission, but added a fluid coupling (a predecessor to today's torque converter) between the engine and clutch. The fluid coupling allowed the car to come to a stop and accelerate away in any gear without using the clutch, which was only needed to shift between gears. Fluid Drive was offered in several variations during the 1950s under a variety of names, including Fluid-Matic (Chrysler), Fluid Drive with Tip-Toe Shift (DeSoto), and Gyro-Matic (Dodge). The low-price Plymouth didn't get a version until 1953. **2.** On the Chrysler Corporation ladder, DeSoto stood just below the top-rung Chrysler. Only two series were offered: DeLuxe and Custom. Most versions shared the Chrysler Windsor/Royal body, but had different styling and a smaller 236-cid six. This $2174 Custom sedan was the best seller. **3.** DeSoto's Custom Sportsman two-door hardtop shows off the reverse-slant roofline and three-piece rear window found on all Chrysler Corp. hardtops. **4-5.** A couple of interesting bodies offered by DeSoto were the 139.5-inch-wheelbase, nine-passenger Suburban sedan with suicide (rear-hinged) back doors, and the wood-trimmed wagon.

4

5

1. Dodge was second on the corporate ladder. The popular Meadowbrook sedan sat on a 123.5-inch wheelbase, listed for $1848, and, like all Dodges, came with a 230-cid six. **2.** Wayfarer was Dodge's 115-inch-wheelbase budget line. Top seller was the $1738 two-door sedan. The Wayfarer line also included a business coupe and the Sportabout convertible. Both only had a front bench seat. **3.** Plymouth was Chrysler Corporation's low-price brand that competed directly with Chevrolet and Ford, and was typically the nation's number-three seller behind those two. Plymouths were known as being solid and reliable, and the 118.5-inch wheelbase of all but the low-line Deluxe two-doors allowed for more interior room than Chevys and Fords with their shorter wheelbases. The $2372 Special Deluxe wood-bodied wagon was Plymouth's most expensive car and sold only 2057 copies. These "woodies" would soon be replaced by steel-bodied versions. **4.** Most popular model was the $1629 Special Deluxe sedan. Like all Plymouths, it carried a 218-cubic-inch six. **5.** Deluxe two-door models sat on a 111-inch wheelbase. Representing the cheapest Plymouth offered for 1950 was this $1371 Deluxe business coupe.

1

2

3

4

5

SCORECARD		1950
MAKE	TOTAL PRODUCTION	RANK
CHRYSLER	179,299 ▲	10th ▲
DE SOTO	133,854 ▲	12th ▲
DODGE	341,797 ▲	7th ▲
PLYMOUTH	610,954 ▲	4th ▼

1

1. Chryslers got a sloped nose and broad, straight-bar grille for 1951, but appearance changes took a distant back seat to the year's mechanical refinements. This big, flashy New Yorker convertible set its buyer back nearly $4000. **2-3.** By far Chrysler's biggest news of the year was the introduction of the powerful hemi-head V-8, which would soon become a legend. Nicknamed for its hemispherically shaped combustion chambers, the "Hemi" featured large valves flanking a centrally mounted spark plug that helped produce complete, even-burning combustion. In its debut season, the Hemi displaced 331 cubic inches and produced a whopping 180 horsepower. Cadillac's V-8 of the same displacement only produced 160. The Hemi powered all models save the base Windsor, which carried over its 250-cid six. The quickest Chrysler was the lightweight Saratoga, which won the stock class in the 1951 Mexican Road Race. **4.** Chrysler offered its first steel-bodied station wagons for 1950; they were sold alongside wood-bodied wagons, which were introduced in mid 1949. By '51, the woodies were gone. The remaining steel-bodied versions were given the Town & Country designation—a name that previously graced a wood-paneled two-door hardtop.

2

4

1

2

3

4

1-2. Topping Chrysler's standard line was the luxurious Imperial. Shown is the most expensive model, the $4402 convertible. Its padded leather-covered dashtop—termed the Safety Crash Pad—was an industry first. **3.** Crown Imperials rode a longer wheelbase and came only as eight-passenger sedans priced in the $6600 range. Fewer than 500 were sold. **4.** DeSoto got Chrysler's sloping nose for 1951, but not its Hemi engine—at least, not yet. For now, buyers had to make do with an enlarged 250-cubic-inch six. DeSoto's toothy grille became a favorite of the custom-car crowd.

1

2

3

4

1-2. Dodges also got a sloped hood for 1951, along with a simpler grille. The bottom-line Wayfarer convertible and two-door sedan each cost around $1930. **3.** By contrast, Plymouth's cheapest convertible was the $2222 Cranbrook. Plymouth was a less prestigious make than Dodge, but this car offered a rear seat that the Wayfarer ragtop didn't—along with a few extra amenities. **4.** Plymouths were low-cost cars, yet it was the line-topping $1826 Cranbrook sedan that sold the best. A midline Cambridge sedan cost about $100 less; the low-line Concord series didn't offer a sedan.

SCORECARD		1951
MAKE	TOTAL PRODUCTION	RANK
CHRYSLER	163,613 ▼	11th ▼
DESOTO	106,000 ▼	15th ▼
DODGE	290,000 ▼	7th ●
PLYMOUTH	611,000 ▲	3rd ▲

the *Beautiful Chrysler*

NEW YORKER AND NEW YORKER DELUXE MODELS

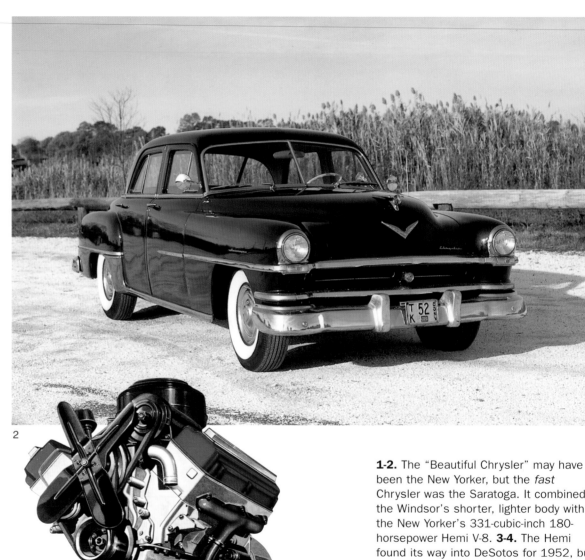

DeSoto
FireDome 8

You've heard about its amazing 160 h.p. V-8 performance...*Full* Power Steering, Power Braking and America's finest No-Shift Driving. Now go and try it for *yourself*! Today!

1
2
3
4

1-2. The "Beautiful Chrysler" may have been the New Yorker, but the *fast* Chrysler was the Saratoga. It combined the Windsor's shorter, lighter body with the New Yorker's 331-cubic-inch 180-horsepower Hemi V-8. **3-4.** The Hemi found its way into DeSotos for 1952, but in a smaller form: 276 cid and 160 hp. Otherwise, the '52 DeSoto was so much like the '51 version that Chrysler Corp. didn't even keep separate sales figures.

"but darling... they're staring at our new '52 Dodge"

Drive the very new, very beautiful '52 Dodge

Enjoy greater all 'round visibility, smoother riding, extra roominess, the pride and satisfaction of having spent your money wisely and well.

Big, new, dependable '52 DODGE

1

"My, the neighbors sure like our New '52 Dodge!"

Let the "Show Down" Way show you why Dodge is so popular

This smart, new Dodge wins admirers with its looks . . . wins hearts with its dependable day-in, day-out performance. You get modern styling—advanced engineering that protects your investment for years ahead. Among its many exciting features is the amazing Dodge Oriflow Ride that makes every mile you travel boulevard-smooth. And if you think this is just sales talk—your Dodge dealer can give you proof! Before you buy a car in any price class, ask him for a free copy of the "Show Down" Plan. It lets you compare Dodge feature by feature against other cars for greater driving ease, comfort and safety . . . greater value. Once you've made this comparison test, we're sure you'll see why "You could pay hundreds of dollars more and still not get all Dodge gives you!"

Specifications and Equipment Subject to Change Without Notice

Big, new, dependable '52 DODGE

2

1. Indeed, most folks would *have* to stare at a '52 Dodge—if they wanted to see any differences from '51. Only detail changes marked the new model year. 2. In the conformity of quickly expanding suburbia, neighbors' opinions mattered. Ad writers assured potential buyers that a $2908 Coronet Sierra station wagon would meet with everyone's approval. 3. Plymouth likewise didn't change much for 1952—unless you consider including the make's name above the trunklid handle a major alteration. 4. Material shortages prompted by the Korean War resulted in lower production—and higher prices. This virtually unchanged Cranbrook convertible went up by more than $100 to $2329. Prices would be rolled back for '53.

3

4

SCORECARD		1952
MAKE	TOTAL PRODUCTION	RANK
CHRYSLER	87,470 ▼	12th ▼
DE SOTO	88,000 ▼	13th ▲
DODGE	206,000 ▼	7th ●
PLYMOUTH	396,000 ▼	3rd ●

1. All Chryslers received a one-piece windshield for 1953. Air conditioning was newly optional, joined late in the model year by Chrysler's first automatic transmission, the two-speed PowerFlite. Just over 2500 New Yorker Newport hardtop coupes were sold at $3487. **2.** Though Chrysler was best known for its powerful Hemi V-8, the make's biggest seller for 1953 was the six-cylinder Windsor series. And the best-selling Windsor was the $2691 Deluxe four-door sedan. **3.** Conspicuous by its absence from this ad is the performance-oriented midline Saratoga, which was dropped for 1953; oddly, the name would reappear a few years later. Imperial isn't mentioned either, but it remained in the lineup.

1

2

3

1

2

1-2. Imperials sat on a longer wheelbase than Windsor and New Yorker, giving them a distinctive—and distinguished—look. The $4225 four-door sedan was the most popular, yet sold only 7800 copies. **3-4.** DeSoto again showed a toothy grille for 1953. Like all Chrysler Corp. cars, it got a one-piece windshield; unlike some of the others (Dodge and Plymouth), it benefited from optional air conditioning. Six-cylinder models were called Powermasters, V-8s were Firedomes. **5.** This $3114 Firedome convertible sports the wire wheels that were offered on all Chrysler Corp. cars for '53.

3

5

4

1-3. Engineering advancements tended to trickle down the corporate ladder, and, for 1953, the Hemi V-8 trickled down to Dodge. Predictably, it was smaller than those fitted to Chryslers and DeSotos. Called the Red Ram, it displaced 241 cubic inches and made 140 horsepower. What hadn't yet trickled down was an automatic transmission; the best Dodge could offer was its semiautomatic Gyro-Torque Drive, a variation of Fluid Drive. **4.** Along with the V-8 came a new model name: Coronet. It also brought a new ram's-head hood ornament, which would be revived during the 1980s for the company's trucks. The only convertible offered was the $2494 Coronet.

1

3

2

extra **Power**

It's like money in the bank! Even when you're not using it, nice to know it's there . . . this surge of

CORONET V-EIGHT CLUB COUPE

New-All New '53 Dodge

The Action Car For Active Americans

In the new 140-h.p. Red Ram V-Eight engine, Dodge engineers have provided you with a magnificent reserve of acceleration and performance. You take to the highway with greater confidence, greater safety. And with this surging Red Ram power, you enjoy nimble change-of-pace of new Gyro-Torque Drive. A new road-hugging, curve-holding ride. A new sense of driving mastery. If your active life demands an Action Car . . . this sleek, trim Dodge is for you. "Road Test" it . . . soon.

4

1

2

3

4

1. Though it wore a one-piece windshield and optional wire wheels for 1953 like its corporate brothers, bottom-rung Plymouth had yet to get a V-8—or even a semiautomatic transmission. That put it at a disadvantage in the low-price field, so late in the model year, Plymouth finally got a version of Fluid Drive called Hy-Drive. By far the best seller of the line was the $1873 Cranbrook four-door sedan. **2.** Though the lowly Plymouth nameplate may have seemed out of place at a ritzy ski lodge, a dressy Cranbrook Belvedere two-door hardtop didn't—and it cost just $2064. **3.** Plymouth offered only two-door station wagons by this time, four-door versions having been dropped after 1950. They were available in both Plymouth lines for that year: the Cambridge ($2064) and dressier Cranbrook ($2207). **4.** Most expensive of all Plymouths for '53 was the $2220 Cranbrook convertible. All Plymouths were powered by the same 217-cubic-inch flathead six used since '42, but it now put out a rousing 100 horsepower.

SCORECARD		1953
MAKE	TOTAL PRODUCTION	RANK
CHRYSLER	170,006 ▲	9th ▲
DeSOTO	130,404 ▲	11th ▲
DODGE	320,008 ▲	7th ●
PLYMOUTH	650,451 ▲	3rd ●

1. Revisions to the grille and headlight bezels gave Chryslers a fresh face for 1954. Horsepower of the Hemi V-8, still at 331 cubic inches, rose from 180 to 195 in New Yorker, and went to 235 in New Yorker Deluxe and Imperial. A flashy New Yorker Deluxe convertible cost a princely $3938. **2.** Windsor was still powered by a 264-cid six with 119 hp, but not for long; this would prove to be the final year for that combination. Windsor prices started at about $2550. **3.** A Town & Country wagon was offered in both the Windsor and New Yorker lines. This New Yorker version cost a sobering $4024—and had predictably low sales. **4.** Listing for well above that was the $4560 Custom Imperial Newport hardtop coupe.

1

The Beautiful *Chrysler* WINDSOR DELUXE

THE BIG CAR IN THE MEDIUM PRICE FIELD

2

3

4

1. Availability of Chrysler Corporation's two-speed PowerFlite automatic transmission was expanded to the lesser lines for 1954, making it an option for this Hemi-powered DeSoto Firedome Sportsman hardtop coupe. **2.** A special-edition DeSoto Coronado boasted extra chrome trim and dressy interior. **3.** Royal was added as Dodge's new top-line series for 1954. Low-line Meadowbrook and midline Coronet were available with either a 110-horsepower six or a 140-hp Hemi V-8, but the Royal was V-8 only. This $2503 Royal hardtop displays a distinctive two-tone paint scheme that was predictive of what would arrive for '55. **4.** Dodge's lightweight, Hemi-powered cars were quite successful in racing, and a Royal 500 convertible paced the Indy 500 that year. To capitalize on this honor, Dodge released 701 replicas. Factory options included PowerFlite automatic transmission for $189, power steering for $134, and Airtemp air conditioning for $643.

1

3

4

2

3

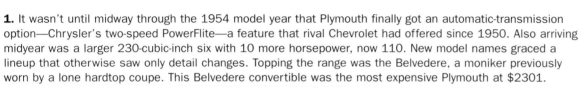
4

1

1. It wasn't until midway through the 1954 model year that Plymouth finally got an automatic-transmission option—Chrysler's two-speed PowerFlite—a feature that rival Chevrolet had offered since 1950. Also arriving midyear was a larger 230-cubic-inch six with 10 more horsepower, now 110. New model names graced a lineup that otherwise saw only detail changes. Topping the range was the Belvedere, a moniker previously worn by a lone hardtop coupe. This Belvedere convertible was the most expensive Plymouth at $2301.
2. Unlike the lower-line Plaza and Savoy, all Belvederes except the wagon wore little tacked-on chrome tailfins. The four-door sedan went for $1953. **3.** Belvedere sport coupes shared the two-tone beltline dip of the convertibles. This version also wears optional wire wheels and continental kit. **4.** Note the exposed tailgate hinges on the finless $2288 Belvedere Suburban two-door wagon.

SCORECARD		1954
MAKE	TOTAL PRODUCTION	RANK
CHRYSLER	105,030 ▼	9th ●
DE SOTO	76,580 ▼	12th ▼
DODGE	154,648 ▼	8th ▼
PLYMOUTH	463,148 ▼	3rd ●

1-2. Virgil Exner took over Chrysler Corporation's styling department in the late Forties, and the redesigned '55 models were the first to show off his radical Forward Look. And radical it was, particularly when compared to the rather dowdy appearance for which the corporation had become known. Topping the Chrysler line was the performance-oriented 300, named for its horsepower output—the highest of any Detroit make that year. As such, it led the blossoming "horsepower race," and made Chryslers the dominant force in stock-car racing. At $4110, however, it was a pricey machine for well-heeled performance connoisseurs, and only 1725 were sold. The 300 shared its large, split grille with the Imperial, which was spun off as a separate make for 1955. **3.** A New Yorker Deluxe Newport two-door coupe (shown) shared the 300's body, but carried the standard Chrysler grille and a 250-hp version of the 331-cubic-inch Hemi V-8. It also carried a $3652 sticker price. Windsor Deluxe remained the entry-level series, but its traditional six-cylinder engine was replaced by a 301-cid polyspherical-head V-8 rated at 225/250 hp that was less efficient—and cheaper to build—than the Hemi. **4.** Chrome fins topped tall taillights as Chrysler followed an industry trend. The New Yorker St. Regis two-door hardtop wore different side trim and paint scheme than the Newport, and cost $38 more.

1

2

3

4

1

2

3

1. DeSoto arguably fared even better than Chrysler with its new Exner styling. Fireflite became the new top-rung model, with Firedome relegated to entry-level status. Both were powered by a 291-cubic-inch Hemi V-8 with 185 or 200 horsepower. This Fireflite Sportsman hardtop coupe listed for $2939. **2.** A station wagon was available only in the Firedome series. DeSoto and Dodge offered the industry's first three-tone paint treatments, this wagon's third color being the grey band surrounding the windows. **3.** The "spring special" Fireflite Coronado came only as a four-door sedan with its own black, white, and turquoise tri-tone paint scheme. **4.** DeSotos featured a pleasing dual-pod dash with round gauges set ahead of the driver. **5.** By contrast, Dodge's design spread the gauges across the dash. **6.** Dodge ads for '55 extolled the virtues of the car's New Horizon sweep-around windshield, and promised that its virtues could be yours "for little more than many models of the 'low priced three'"—taking an indirect stab at its own Plymouth stablemate.

4

5

6

1

2

3

4

5

1-2. Dodge's new top-of-the-line series was the Custom Royal, followed by the Royal and Coronet. Only the Coronet was available with the 230-cubic-inch six, now making 123 horsepower. All others came with a 270-cid V-8, though there were two versions: Custom Royals got a Hemi with 183/193 hp, others a non-hemi-head version with 175. A Custom Royal convertible cost $2748; a two-door hardtop was a couple hundred dollars less. **3.** Imperial became a separate make for 1955, but shared its large eggcrate grille with the Chrysler 300. Unique, however, were its "gun sight" taillights perched atop the rear fenders. Power came from the same 331-cid 250-hp Hemi V-8 found in Chryslers. A stately four-door sedan cost $4483. **4.** With no convertible in the line, the most expensive "regular" Imperial was the $4720 Newport hardtop coupe. **5.** The long-wheelbase (149.5 inches) Crown Imperial was sold mainly as a limousine, as its $7000 sticker precluded many personal-car sales.

all-new
'55 PLYMOUTH

1

2

1. Of all Chrysler Corp. makes, Plymouth underwent the greatest transformation for '55. Not only did it boast a striking, modern look, but it also received its first V-8. Called Hy-Fire, the wedge-head engine (it wasn't a Hemi) arrived in two displacements: 241 and 260 cubic inches, with ratings from 157 to 177 horsepower. **2.** Oddly, '55 Plymouths kept the same model names as their dowdy predecessors. Belvedere again topped the lineup, this sport coupe starting at $2217. Three-tone paint schemes weren't offered, but two-tones—in a rather odd pattern—were. **3.** The symmetrical dashboard got round gauges, and when the optional automatic transmission was ordered, it also got a dash-mounted shift lever, referred to in ads as the "PowerFlite Range Selector." **4.** While the cheapest six-cylinder Plaza sedan started at $1781, this top-line Belvedere sedan sold slightly better—at $200 more. **5.** Another Belvedere sedan was chosen as a test mule for an experimental turbine-engine conversion. It never made production, but it became the first turbine-powered car to be driven on American streets.

3

4

5

SCORECARD		1955
MAKE	TOTAL PRODUCTION	RANK
CHRYSLER	152,777 ▲	9th ●
DeSOTO	114,765 ▲	13th ▼
DODGE	276,936 ▲	8th ●
IMPERIAL	11,432 ▲	17th
PLYMOUTH	401,075 ▲	6th ▼

1

2

3

4

5

6

1. "Power Style" Chryslers wore taller tailfins for 1956, courtesy of a facelift that actually improved upon the '55 redesign. **2.** New Yorker's Hemi V-8 was enlarged to 354 cubic inches, bringing 280 horses along for the ride. Chrysler joined DeSoto and Dodge in offering three-tone paint combinations, as shown on this $3931 New Yorker Newport hardtop coupe. **3.** Windsor—like New Yorker, now minus the "Deluxe" surname—was again the entry-level Chrysler, and the $2870 Windsor sedan was again the top-selling model. Joining the four-door sedan was a new four-door hardtop (in both Windsor and New Yorker trim), which did away with the sedan's center roof pillar. Windsors also got a displacement increase for '56, now with a 331-cid V-8 making 225 or 250 hp. **4.** Chrysler's mighty 300 returned for 1956 with even more muscle. Newly named the 300-B, its 354 Hemi was tuned for 340 horsepower in standard form, 355 with optional dual four-barrel carburetors—making it the first American car to boast one horsepower per cubic inch, a long-standing target for efficiency. Still, the $4419 300-B was an expensive specialty car that garnered a mere 1102 orders. **5.** All '56 Chrysler Corp. cars with automatic transmission traded their dash-mounted shift levers for now-famous pushbuttons mounted in a pod on the left side of the dashboard. There was no Park button, so the parking brake got a workout. **6.** An unusual Chrysler option was Highway Hi Fi, a record player mounted beneath the center of the dashboard. It played special seven-inch records at 16⅔ rpm.

1-3. DeSoto got its own "halo car" for 1956 in the form of the gold-trimmed Adventurer. DeSoto's standard V-8 grew to 330 cubic inches and 230/255 horsepower for '56, but the Adventurer got a 341-cid version good for 320 hp. Adventurer copied the flavor of Chrysler's 300-B, but at a significantly lower price—$3728 vs. $4419—yet fewer than 1000 were sold. **4.** A new body style introduced in all Chrysler Corp. makes for '56 was the four-door hardtop sedan. Lacking a middle roof pillar gave it the sportier look of a two-door hardtop while maintaining the easier rear-seat access of a four-door. This stunning Fireflite Sportsman hardtop sedan started at $3431. It's equipped with optional air conditioning—which was mounted in the trunk—as evidenced by the small scoop beside the rear roof pillar and the cold-air outlet behind the rear seat. On a historical note, it was a Fireflite convertible that paced the Indy 500 in 1956—the only time a DeSoto was so honored.

1

2

DE SOTO presents the

320 hp

golden ADVENTURER

Daring performance *in a setting of* distinguished elegance

From the golden flash of its hubcaps to its golden-hued interior, the new De Soto Adventurer displays a classic elegance that rivals even the legendary cars built for kings, potentates and maharajas. But here is far more than exquisite craftsmanship . . . here is a car with performance to match supreme luxury.

The Adventurer has a 320 horsepower engine to give wings to its beauty. And it has all the other fabulous De Soto features . . . push-button drive selector . . . Full-Time Power Steering* . . . super-highway brakes . . . Airtemp air conditioning* . . . and hi-fi record player*.

'56 DE SOTO—for the super-highway age!

3

4

1

2

3

4

5

6

7

1-2. Dodge flexed its muscles for '56 with the potent D-500 option. It brought the newly enlarged 315-cubic-inch Super Red Ram V-8, but fitted it with a four-barrel carburetor for 230 horsepower—or 260 with high-compression heads. D-500 was optional on all models, and turned the lightweight Dodge into a fearsome street performer. **3.** In what was becoming an annual event, Dodge's "spring special" for '56 was the Golden Lancer, a trim package for the top-line Custom Royal Lancer hardtop coupe. A crossed-flag "500" insignia on the trunk identified the D-500 option. **4.** "The Magic Touch of Tomorrow" was Dodge's announcement of new pushbutton activation for its automatic transmission. Not mentioned in the ad was Dodge's equally new four-door hardtop sedan. **5.** The lowest-priced Dodge was a Coronet two-door sedan, which started at $2194 in six-cylinder form. It was also available with a 270-cid 189-hp V-8 for $103 more. **6.** Wagons were offered as the two-door Suburban or four-door Sierra. For cost reasons, '56 wagons retained the '55 rear-end treatment. **7.** Imperial kept its "gun sight" taillights for '56, which now sat atop taller fins. Underhood was Chrysler's 354 Hemi with 280 hp, but backing it was a new three-speed automatic, the first of the legendary TorqueFlites.

1

2

3

1. Like its corporate brothers, Plymouths wore taller tailfins for '56. Also like its stablemates, the available V-8 engines grew in size and power. The former 241- and 260-cubic-inch V-8s were replaced by 270- and 277-cid units with 180-200 horsepower. Still standard on most models was a 230-cid six, now with 125 hp. A top-line Belvedere convertible listed for $2478. **2-3.** Two- and four-door wagons were grouped under the Suburban model name for '56. This line-topping $2484 Suburban Sport shows off that year's new taillight treatment. **4.** A midyear arrival was the aptly named Fury. Offered only in white with gold anodized trim, the Fury was fitted with a 240-hp 303-cid V-8 that powered it to a couple of stock-car records—certainly not the kind of achievement usually associated with stodgy old Plymouth. It made such an impact that the Fury name continued to grace Plymouth models through the end of the 1980s.

4

SCORECARD		1956
MAKE	TOTAL PRODUCTION	RANK
CHRYSLER	128,322 ▼	10th ▼
DESOTO	110,418 ▼	11th ▲
DODGE	240,686 ▼	8th ●
IMPERIAL	10,684 ▼	17th ●
PLYMOUTH	552,577 ▲	4th ▲

1

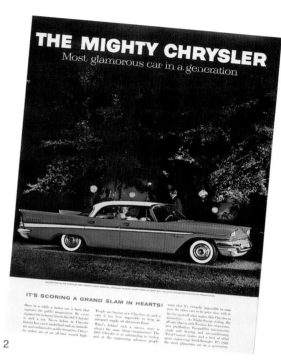

1. The second generation of Virgil Exner's Forward Look caused a sensation when the 1957 models hit showrooms. They indeed looked futuristic with their flowing lines and tall fins, and, where legal, many sported quad headlights. Not surprisingly, engines grew once again; the Hemi used in New Yorkers was now a 392 with 325 horsepower. Newly available was the three-speed TorqueFlite automatic transmission introduced the previous year on Imperials. Also new was torsion-bar front suspension. A New Yorker coupe went for $4202. **2.** The usual ad rhetoric notwithstanding, it's difficult to imagine such praise—"Most glamorous car in a generation"—being lavished on the boxy Chryslers of just three years before. **3-4.** Perhaps even more glamorous than the four-door sedan in the ad was this $4638 New Yorker convertible. Oddly, just 1049 were sold.

2

3

4

2

1

1-3. Chrysler's muscular 300-C (the letter suffix would take one step up the alphabet every year) got a unique grille for '57 rather than sharing it with the Imperial. Its engine again topped those of lesser Chryslers, offering 375 horsepower in base form, 390 optionally—both with dual four-barrel carburetors, which were sported by all of the "letter series" cars until 1964. A convertible was offered for the first time, yet drew only 484 orders at its steep $5359 starting price. **4.** Faring even worse saleswise was the 300's counterpart over at sister division DeSoto. Built on the same size wheelbase, the Adventurer had to "make do" with 345 hp from a 345-cubic-inch Hemi. A mere 300 convertible versions were sold at $4272—more than a grand less than a comparable 300-C.

3

4

1

2

3

4

5

6

7

1. To distinguish them from lesser DeSotos, Adventurers wore a headlight treatment similar to that used on the Chrysler 300-C. The coupe version cost $3997 and sold 1650 copies. **2.** Firesweep was DeSoto's lowest trim level, but you wouldn't know it by the look of this $3169 Shopper station wagon. It could be ordered with a rear-facing third-row seat. **3.** Non-Adventurer DeSotos got the front-end treatment of this Firesweep coupe; the example shown has the dual headlights still required in some states for the '57 model year. Firesweeps had a 325-cubic-inch V-8 with up to 260 horsepower, Firedome and Fireflite a 341 with up to 290 hp. **4.** "Swept-Wing" styling graced Dodges for 1957. A six-cylinder engine was still offered, but few Dodges were purchased that way; most had a 325-cid V-8 with up to 310 hp. **5-6.** This Coronet Lancer coupe started at $2580, but was optioned with the top D-500 engine, a 354 Hemi V-8 with 340 hp. **7.** Dodge prices started at $2370 for a six-cylinder two-door sedan; fitting it with a V-8 cost $108 more. Like all '57 Chrysler Corp. cars, torsion-bar front suspension was standard, a three-speed TorqueFlite automatic transmission optional.

1

2

3

4

1. For 1957, Imperial got its first distinct bodyshell; previously, it shared one with Chrysler models. Incorporated in the design was the first use of curved side glass in an American car. Not incorporated, but available as an option, was a fake spare tire cover for the trunklid. It proved popular, but in later years would be derided as the "toilet seat." Gun sight taillights remained, but were now set into the trailing edges of tall fins. A Crown convertible started at $5598. **2-3.** A Crown four-door—whether in hardtop or sedan form—went for $5406. Crown was the midline series now, LeBaron being installed as the top-line model. **4.** Filling out the range of body styles offered is this $5269 Crown Southampton coupe. All Imperials came with the same 325-horsepower 392 Hemi used in most Chryslers.

1

1. "In one flaming moment, Plymouth leaps three full years ahead." Indeed, styling of all Chrysler Corp. cars looked futuristic for '57, but it was perhaps least expected on the low-price Plymouth. 2. A $2638 Belvedere convertible shows off the year's revised dashboard. 3. A Belvedere four-door hardtop cost $109 more than a comparable four-door sedan, but many felt the sleeker look well worth the money. The 277-cubic-inch V-8 returned, but was joined by a 301-cid version with up to 235 horsepower. 4-5. Topping the Plymouth line was again the white-hot Fury, again offered in only one color combination. New, however, was a 318-cid V-8 with 290 hp.

2

4

3

5

SCORECARD		1957
MAKE	TOTAL PRODUCTION	RANK
CHRYSLER	124,675 ▾	10th ●
DESOTO	117,514 ▴	11th ●
DODGE	287,608 ▴	7th ▴
IMPERIAL	37,593 ▴	15th ▴
PLYMOUTH	762,231 ▴	3rd ▴

1. A 1958 recession hit the little-changed Chryslers pretty hard. The company fought back with a "spring special" Windsor Dartline, but in the end, Chrysler sales totaled about half those of 1957. **2-3.** Grilles were altered slightly, taillight lenses were shorter, and most engines gained a few horsepower, but Chrysler offered little new for '58 to entice buyers. **4-5.** The letter series took its usual step up the alphabetical ladder, but the 300-D was a virtual rerun of the 300-C.

2

3

4

5

1

2

3

4

5

6

7

1-3. DeSotos changed even less than their Chrysler siblings for '58, and quite predictably, sales dropped even more. A boost in engine displacement from 325/341 cubic inches to 350/361 cid probably didn't help during recessionary '58, when fuel economy suddenly became a concern—enough so to encourage the Big Three to develop the compacts that would appear for 1960. As it turned out, it marked the beginning of the end for poor DeSoto. **4.** Faring slightly better was Dodge, which though also little-changed, still offered a frugal six-cylinder engine—and, of course, lower prices. With little else to tout, a "New Spring Swept-Wing" was released midyear with "Breathtaking new colors" and "Bewitching new interiors." **5-7.** In an odd reversal of recent trends, the hot-rod D-500 option actually *lost* horsepower for '58 (gasp!) thanks to a switch from a 354 Hemi V-8 to a less efficient—but cheaper—361 "wedge-head." The top-rated engine dropped seven hp to 333.

1

1-2. If you liked the 1957 Imperial, you'd probably like the '58 as well. In fact, you'd probably be hard-pressed to tell them apart. In what was otherwise a nearly standpat year, horsepower rose by 20, prices by about $100. This Crown two-door hardtop went for $5388.
3. Though the flashier hardtop sedan cost the same, about a third of four-door buyers bought the traditional pillared sedan. In the midline Crown series, it cost $5632.

2

3

1

2

3

1. Though "new" appears four times in this ad copy, there really wasn't much that was on 1958 Plymouths. An exception was a larger 350-cubic-inch V-8 optional on all models (instead of just the top-line Fury coupe) that made 305 horsepower, or 315 with the very rare—and rather unreliable—fuel injection. **2.** The Belvedere line offered Plymouth's classiest hardtop sedan for $2528. Whether two doors or four, hardtops cost about $70-$90 more than comparable pillared bodies. **3.** The most popular Plymouth of all was the $2305 Savoy four-door sedan. Engine choices ranged from a thrifty 230-cubic-inch six to the hot-rod fuelie 350, but most were probably sold with a 318-cid V-8 of 225-250 hp.

SCORECARD		1958
MAKE	TOTAL PRODUCTION	RANK
CHRYSLER	63,681 ▼	11th ▼
DESOTO	49,445 ▼	13th ▼
DODGE	137,861 ▼	9th ▼
IMPERIAL	16,133 ▼	16th ▼
PLYMOUTH	443,799 ▼	3rd ●

1. An effective facelift adorned 1959 Chryslers, but the biggest change was underhood, as the mighty Hemi was no more. In its place was a conventional Golden Lion wedge-head V-8 of 383 or 413 cubic inches, which Chrysler justified as "a lighter, more efficient engine designed to give you better performance at the speeds you drive the most." Not mentioned is that it was also a heck-of-a-lot cheaper to build. New options for '59 included speed control, rear air suspension, and a swiveling driver's seat to ease entry. **2.** Pretty in pink, a New Yorker convertible cost $4890 with its standard 413-cid 350-horsepower V-8. **3.** Entry-level Windsors carried a 383-cid V-8 good for 305 hp. This coupe went for $3289. **4.** Like other Chryslers, the 300-E lost its Hemi engine, but the 413-cid wedge-head that replaced it put out about the same horsepower: 380 standard, 390 optionally. The E carried over the D's front-end styling, but wore the new '59 tail treatment. By this time, sales were down to a trickle, at just 550 of the $5319 hardtops, and only 140 of the $5749 convertibles.

1

3

2

4

1

2

1-3. In a year when other Chrysler Corp. makes were up slightly, DeSoto sales continued to drop. Though somewhat higher for 1959, a total of 697 Adventurer orders could hardly be considered encouraging. Furthermore, the Adventurer was now a little less special; previously, it had always carried a more powerful engine than other DeSotos, but for '59, its 383-cubic-inch, 350-horsepower V-8 was also available on lesser models—and lower-priced Dodges. 4-5. Speaking of Dodge, a new face graced the '59s, with heavily chromed eyebrows and a large loop bumper surrounding a mesh grille. Revised styling was "pointier" at each end, giving the car a more exaggerated look. This top-line Custom Royal Lancer coupe went for $3201.

3

4

5

1

2

3

1. Dodge wagons came in Custom and Sierra trim with six- or nine-passenger seating. Tailfin styling carried over from '58—and '57—and the bodies were shared by DeSoto and Plymouth. Prices ranged from $3103 to $3439. **2.** V-8 choices included a 326 cubic incher with 255 horsepower, a 361 with 295-305 hp, and the new 383 shared with DeSoto that put out 320 hp in D-500 form, 345 in Super D-500 tune—which is the engine powering this loaded Custom Royal convertible that started at $3422. **3.** The stately Crown Imperial limousine was the only '59 Chrysler Corp. car to remain powered by a Hemi; even the "civilian" Imperials switched to a wedge-head engine that year. A long-wheelbase sedan/limo had been offered by Chrysler since the early '30s, but sales had slowed to a trickle by this time, partly due to a staggering price: $15,075—more than three times that of a base Imperial. This is one of only seven '59s built. Surprisingly, the Crown Imperial continued into the mid 1960s, never selling more than 16 a year. **4.** A heavy, chromed grille and new headlight treatment distinguished the '59 Imperial. Power came from a 413-cubic-inch V-8 delivering 350 hp. The least expensive model in the line was this Custom Southampton coupe at $4910. **5.** At 129 inches, a $5774 Imperial Crown convertible rode a three-inch-longer wheelbase than its Chrysler New Yorker counterpart, giving it impressive stature.

4

5

1

2

1. Plymouth indeed got most of what was new at Chrysler Corp. for 1959. Back ends changed more than fronts, but the overall look was decidedly different than '58's. Hardtops and convertibles shared a compound-curve windshield that wrapped over at the top. Options included swivel bucket seats along with the fake spare tire cover introduced on Imperials the year before. **2-3.** Sport Fury became the new top-line model for '59, offered only in hardtop coupe and convertible form priced at $2927 and $3125, respectively. Horsepower was curbed a bit for 1959, as the 318-cubic-inch V-8 standard in Sport Fury was tamed to 260, down 30 from its '58 peak. A new 361-cid V-8 replaced the 350 as optional, but produced the same 305 hp in carbureted form—and wasn't offered with '58's fuel injection. **4.** This 1959 Chrysler family portrait found the corporation in much the same position as it entered the decade, with offerings spanning the price spectrum from the low-price Plymouth to the high-end Imperial. Sadly, both of those makes have since departed: Imperial after 1975 (though the name would pop up now and again on luxury models of various descriptions), Plymouth in the early '00s, after being considered redundant—and inferior—to Dodge. Beating them both to the grave was DeSoto, which was celebrating its 30th anniversary as this photo was taken; it would not survive to celebrate its 33rd. Today, only Dodge and Chrysler remain—the two makes that originally merged under Walter P. Chrysler to form Chrysler Corp. in the late 1920s.

3

4

SCORECARD		1959
MAKE	TOTAL PRODUCTION	RANK
CHRYSLER	69,970 ▲	12th ▼
DESOTO	45,724 ▼	13th ●
DODGE	156,385 ▲	8th ▲
IMPERIAL	17,269 ▲	17th ▼
PLYMOUTH	458,259 ▲	3rd ●

While Henry Ford didn't invent the automobile, his Model T of 1909-1927 was certainly instrumental in bringing it to the masses. Also monumental was the debut of Ford's famous flathead V-8 in 1932, an engine that would power the company's cars for two decades and become a favorite among hot-rodders.

In an effort to expand its market presence, Ford Motor Company purchased the luxury Lincoln brand in 1922, and brought out the midpriced Mercury nameplate for 1939. Though both were reasonably successful, overall sales and corporation profits went on the decline during the Forties, and the huge conglomerate that was Ford Motor Company found itself teetering on the brink of collapse.

As Ford entered the 1950s, it was digging out of its financial hole on the strength of its redesigned 1949 models, which helped Ford beat Chevrolet in the production race for only the second time since 1938. Through the rest of the decade, it usually ran a very close runner-up; and with the exception of the ill-fated Edsel, Ford Motor Company made the right moves to set it up for the 1960s and beyond.

2

3

4

1

5

6

7

8

1. Henry Ford II (center), sometimes called "Henry the Deuce," took the reins of Ford Motor Company from his father in 1945. He hired a group of young engineers and executives known as the "Whiz Kids" to turn the ailing company around. Their efforts resulted in the redesigned 1949 models. **2.** The '49 proved so successful (thereby saving Ford's bacon) that it wasn't altered much for 1950. Though Tudor (proper spelling) models were more popular, Fordor (also proper spelling) versions sold strongly, with prices starting at $1472. Buyers had a choice of a 226-cubic-inch 95-horsepower six or the venerable 239-cid 100-hp flathead V-8. Both were offered only with manual transmission. Ford competed against Chevrolet and Plymouth, a trio known as the "low-priced three." **3.** Deluxe and Custom trim levels were offered for 1950, but only the latter had a convertible, which was priced at $1886. **4.** The wood-bodied two-door Country Squire wagon was claimed to carry "8 big people in comfort" for $2119. **5.** Ford didn't have a two-door hardtop to compete with Chevy's stylish new Bel Air, so at midyear it released a special Tudor, the two-tone vinyl-topped $1711 Crestliner. **6.** Lincoln competed in the luxury segment with Cadillac and Chrysler Imperial, falling between the two in sales. Prices started at $2529 for this base coupe. All Lincolns shared a 336-cid 154-hp flathead V-8. Newly optional was Hydra-Matic automatic transmission, which Lincoln purchased from General Motors. **7.** Lincoln's upper-crust Cosmopolitan rode a four-inch-longer wheelbase and featured distinctive front wheelwell "eyebrows." This $3240 Sport Sedan shows off its "suicide" rear doors. **8.** Mercurys played in the midprice field against the likes of DeSoto and Oldsmobile. Like their Ford siblings, Mercs were redesigned for 1949, and were equally successful. They were powered by a 239-cid version of the flathead V-8 rated at 110 hp. A Mercury similar to this $2412 convertible paced the 1950 Indy 500. **9.** Mercury coupes became a favorite of the hot-rod set, particularly after staring as James Dean's ride in the movie *Rebel Without a Cause*.

9

SCORECARD		1950
MAKE	TOTAL PRODUCTION	RANK
FORD	1,208,912 ▲	2nd ▼
LINCOLN	28,190 ▼	16th ▲
MERCURY	293,658 ▼	9th ▼

1-2. For 1951, Ford finally got a hardtop to compete with Chevy's Bel Air—and the new Plymouth Belvedere. Called the Victoria, it came only with a V-8 for $1925. **3.** Ford also caught up with Chevy in the transmission race with fully automatic Ford-O-Matic. Chevy had introduced the Powerglide for 1950; Plymouth wouldn't get an automatic until '54. The '51 Fords got a revised grille that replaced the former central "spinner" with two smaller ones, as shown on this $1553 Custom Fordor sedan. **4.** Looking right at home in this beach scene is a $2029 Country Squire "woody" wagon.

1

2

3

1. The most expensive ship in Lincoln's 1951 fleet was the $3891 Cosmopolitan convertible. Note the revised side trim, which was now shared with lesser Lincolns. 2-3. The most popular Lincoln was the base $2553 Sport Sedan. 4-5. A dressy Capri edition of the Cosmopolitan two-door coupe brought "the ultimate in fine-car styling and coach work"—all for just $3350. 6. A similarly dressed version of the base Lincoln coupe was the $2702 Lido.

4

5

6

1

2

3

1. Nineteen fifty-one would prove to be the final year for Mercury's two-door woody wagon. At $2530, it carried the loftiest list price of any '51 Merc. **2.** Mercury got its own version of Ford's fully automatic Ford-O-Matic transmission for 1951 called—you guessed it—Merc-O-Matic. It was a big deal to Mercury dealers, who had been losing business to "automatic" rivals. **3.** Buyers could purchase a Mercury coupe for as little as $1947. By contrast, the local Ford dealer could sell a Tudor for about $500 less.

SCORECARD		1951
MAKE	TOTAL PRODUCTION	RANK
FORD	1,013,381 ▼	2nd ●
LINCOLN	32,574 ▲	18th ▼
MERCURY	310,387 ▲	6th ▲

1

2

1. A string of brand spankin' new 1952 Fords are shown rolling off the Dearborn assembly line. **2.** Ford Motor Company was the only corporation to restyle all of its cars for 1952. But Ford ads pointed out that a fresh look wasn't the only thing that was new. A reengineered 215-cubic-inch overhead-valve Mileage Maker six was smaller in displacement than the previous six, but at 101 horsepower, had more guts. Meanwhile, the 239-cid flathead V-8 added ten ponies for a total of 110.

1

2

3

1-2. Some felt Ford's 1949 restyle hadn't yet worn out its welcome, but the '52 models truly looked advanced. Returning from 1950 was the central-mounted grille spinner, but the rest of the car was unmistakably new, with a squared-up profile and protruding head- and taillights. A Crestline Victoria hardtop coupe cost $1925. **2.** For another $102, a Crestline buyer could go topless. **3.** Ford's first all-steel wagons appeared for 1952, but they weren't cheap: a Country Squire was $2186.

1-2. Sales didn't reflect it, but Lincoln was all new for '52. Aside from its vertical taillights, it reflected the same styling themes as its humble Ford stablemate— which may have been part of the problem. But it also got a new 317-cubic-inch overhead-valve V-8 with 160 horsepower, and that was definitely *not* part of the problem: This engine powered a quartet of Lincolns to a 1-2-3-4 finish in the grueling *Carrera Panamericana* road race, a truly amazing feat. Capri was now the top-line model, the convertible version of which sold for $3665. **3.** Cosmopolitan became the entry-level Lincoln, this four-door sedan being the cheapest at $3198. Added to both lines was a new two-door hardtop.

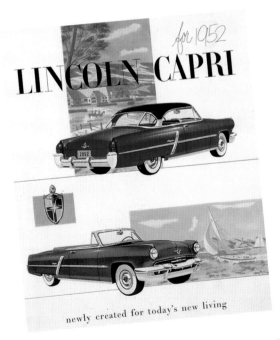

LINCOLN CAPRI

for 1952

newly created for today's new living

1

2

3

1

Stretch Out and See

Why It Challenges Them All

NEW SPACE-PLANNED DESIGN—No unused space—this is the new lean-back-and-take-it-easy Mercury that puts every inch of car to work. And look! "Forerunner" styling is years ahead.

WE BUILT A NEW CAR and made this challenge: Match Mercury if you can. Now we know we've got the sweetest thing on wheels since the ladies began to drive.

For all America is falling in love with a car.

No wonder. It's big and beautiful, inside, outside, and all over. With a host of Future Features—Forerunner styling, Jet-scoop hood, suspension-mounted brake pedal, Interceptor instrument panel, higher horsepower V-8 engine—the new Mercury is the most challenging car that ever came down the *American Road.*

See it, drive it. You'll fall in love, too. And with Mercury's famous economy—proved in official tests—this is a love affair you can afford.

MERCURY DIVISION • FORD MOTOR COMPANY

The New 19**52**

MERCURY

WITH MERC-O-MATIC DRIVE

3-WAY CHOICE—Mercury presents three dependable, performance-proved drives: silent-ease, standard transmission, thrifty Touch-O-Matic Overdrive,* and Merc-O-Matic,* greatest of all automatic drives.
*Optional at extra cost.

3

SWEEPSTAKES WINNER OF MOBILGAS ECONOMY RUN...
There can be only one big winner in this annual automobile classic. And again this year it was Mercury with optional overdrive—the all-time economy champion, with two Sweepstakes wins against all comers in every class, and three wins in three years against every car entered in its own class.

can't be beaten for economy
...won't be dated for years!

NEW SEA-TINT* GLASS reduces heat, glare, and eyestrain. New larger windows permit safety-sure visibility all around. Every view proves that Mercury is new—in looks, in power, in extra value.

Standard equipment, accessories, and trim illustrated are subject to change without notice. White-wall tires, when available, at extra cost.

EYE AMERICA'S NO.1 STYLING STAR

MERCURY

TRY "AMERICA'S NO.1 ECONOMY CAR."

What other car has such a record for economy—proven in open competition? Answer: None, as a look at the Mobilgas Economy Run record shows you.

And what other can match Mercury for years-ahead styling and future features? We'll let you answer that one yourself. Just compare Mercury with any car you've seen, or driven. Then—remember these extracts:

Mercury's styling is completely new, not an outmoded, years-ago design that's trying to hide its age. And there's 12% more V-8 horsepower, 17% more visibility, six inches more hip room in the rear seat alone, a new Interceptor panel . . .

But the list is so long! So, all we say is, take your own word for it. There's a car waiting for you to try at your Mercury dealer's. Why not stop in today—and step out for your own private test run!

MERCURY DIVISION • FORD MOTOR COMPANY

2

1. Like Ford, Mercury shifted to all-steel wagons for 1952. For those who had difficulty accepting the transition, both companies offered woodgrain appliqués and trim to soothe their nerves. There were no more two-door wagons, but the four-doors came with a choice of six- or eight-passenger seating. They started at $2525 and $2570, respectively. For '52, the flathead V-8 was coaxed to 125 horses. **2.** A 1952 ad points out that Mercury won its class in the Mobilgas Economy Run—three years in a row. It also claims the cars "won't be dated for years"—probably a safe bet, since they'd just been redesigned. **3.** "We built a new car and made this challenge: Match Mercury if you can," said another ad. Those tough words were met with a huge drop in sales and a fall from sixth place to eighth in the industry. Oops.

SCORECARD		1952
MAKE	TOTAL PRODUCTION	RANK
FORD	671,733 ▼	2nd ●
LINCOLN	27,271 ▼	19th ▼
MERCURY	172,087 ▼	8th ▼

1

2

3

4

1. Fords were treated to a mild facelift for 1953, which would turn out to be the final year for the venerable flathead V-8. And that's what powers this Crestline Sunliner convertible, which started at $2043. **2.** Crestline buyers could opt for a sporty Victoria hardtop at $1941. **3.** This midline $1582 Customline two-door sedan also sports the V-8, which was good for 110 horsepower in its final year. **4.** Ford was putting on a full-court sales press in an effort to catch Chevrolet (it didn't work), and this ad attempted to convey the wisdom in buying two.

1

2

3

1. Only subtle styling changes marked the 1953 Lincolns in a year that brought big changes underhood: Engineers found another 45 horses hiding in the 317-cubic-inch V-8, which now corralled a total of 205. All those ponies could be enjoyed in a Cosmopolitan hardtop for $3322. **2.** This brochure cover shows one of the multicolor interiors available in a Lincoln. **3-4.** Unbelievably, it happened again. For the second year in a row, Lincolns placed 1-2-3-4 in the *Carrera Panamericana* road race.

4

1

2

1. Indeed, one had to "Take a good look" to see any changes in the '53 Mercurys, which got little more than trim revisions. 2. The line was now divided into Custom and top-line Monterey models, the latter hosting this $2390 convertible. 3. A Monterey sedan went for $2133. 4. Henry the Deuce, Benson, and William Clay Ford pose with the 40-millionth Ford vehicle, a Mercury Monterey convertible, during Ford's 50th-anniversary year.

3

4

SCORECARD		1953
MAKE	TOTAL PRODUCTION	RANK
FORD	1,247,542 ▲	2nd ●
LINCOLN	40,762 ▲	17th ▲
MERCURY	305,863 ▲	8th ●

1

2

1. In a year that brought few styling changes of note, Ford redefined the sunroof concept for 1954 with the Crestline Skyliner. Traditional sunroofs—as they're known today—first appeared in the late 1930s, but the Skyliner took a different approach: The whole forward half of the roof was made of tinted glass, and yes, it tended to bake the interior in sunny climates. This model was offered only in the top-line Crestline series for $2164, a $109 price premium over a standard Victoria hardtop. **2.** The biggest change to the 1954 Ford appeared under the hood: After 20 years of faithful service, the flathead V-8 was finally put out to pasture. In its place was a new Y-Block overhead-valve V-8 of the same displacement: 239 cubic inches. As testimony to the added efficiency of the new design, horsepower rose from 110 to 130. **3.** Lincolns likewise looked little different for 1954, and could boast of neither new models nor more power. **4-5.** Mercury offered its own glass-roof model for 1956, the $2582 Monterey Sun Valley. **6.** Mercury styling changes were minimal for '56, but available as an option were bullet front-bumper guards, as shown on this $2610 Monterey convertible. **7.** The least expensive '54 Mercury, a $2194 Custom two-door sedan, is shown wearing the standard front bumper.

3

4

America's first transparent-top car

NEW MERCURY
Sun Valley

5

6

7

SCORECARD		1954
MAKE	TOTAL PRODUCTION	RANK
FORD	1,165,942 ▼	1st ▲
LINCOLN	36,993 ▼	15th ▲
MERCURY	259,305 ▼	7th ▲

1

2

3

4

1. Nineteen fifty-five was a big year for Ford. A complete restyle brought subtle tailfins and a fresh look—plus some unusual two-tone paint schemes. The $2224 Sunliner convertible was now part of the new top-line Fairlane series, which replaced the Crestline. **2.** Also exclusive to the Fairlane series was the $2202 Crown Victoria hardtop, which featured a brushed-metal roof band. The front half of the roof could be converted to tinted glass for an extra $70. **3.** The least expensive Fairlane was the $1914 two-door Club Sedan. Mainline and Customline models could be ordered with an enlarged 272-cubic-inch V-8 with 162 to 182 horsepower, but Fairlanes could be optioned with a 292-cid version with 198 horses. That was nearly double the maximum horsepower offered in a Ford as recently as 1951. **4.** What was called the Country Sedan wasn't a sedan at all, but a wagon with six- or eight-passenger seating. They retailed for $2156 and $2287, respectively. All wagons were now grouped in their own series, which also included the two-door Ranch and four-door Country Squire. **5.** Perhaps Ford's biggest news for 1955 was the introduction of the Thunderbird. The two-seater was intended to go head-to-head with Chevrolet's Corvette, but it was hardly a fair fight: The amply equipped T-Bird outsold the rudimentary—and similarly priced—'Vette by a whopping 23:1 margin. A 292-cubic-inch V-8 good for 193 horsepower (198 with automatic transmission) was standard in the T-Bird. **6.** Ford Motor Company chairman Henry Ford II steps out of a '55 T-Bird. **7-8.** Though it was a two-seat convertible, Ford shied away from calling the Thunderbird a "sports car," instead preferring to call it a "personal car." Available T-Bird amenities included a telescopic steering column, power seat, and lift-off hardtop.

5

6

7

A personal car of distinction...
FORD THUNDERBIRD

8

1

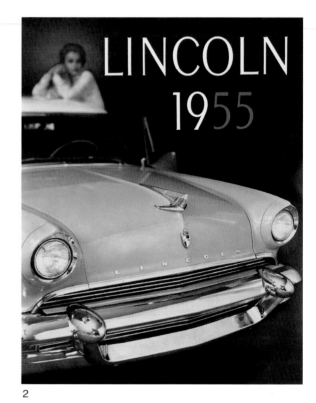

2

3

1. Lincoln underwent a radical makeover for 1955 that made it look longer and sleeker despite an unchanged wheelbase. Much of that was due to extended tailfins capping tall, "cathedral" taillights, coincidentally similar to those adopted by Packard. A top-line Capri convertible—Lincoln's priciest car—cost $4072. **2-3.** "Frenched" headlights encircled in chrome and a simple, horizontal-bar grille gave Lincoln's front end a classier look. So did a stately chrome-and-gold hood ornament. Speaking of the hood, it covered a 341-cubic-inch V-8 rated at 225 horsepower, up from '54's 317 with 205 hp. This 1955 Capri two-door hardtop listed for $3910.

1

2

MERCURY'S NEW MONTCLAIR SERIES

3

4

1. It was easy to recognize the restyled 1955 Mercury thanks to its hooded headlights and revised grille. Monterey was relegated to midline status as Montclair became the top dog. This glass-topped Montclair Sun Valley sold for $2712, about $450 more than its Ford counterpart. **2.** Those who missed the woody wagons of the early '50s could get their $2844 Monterey wagon fitted with wood-grain trim. **3.** The squared-off rear fenders and taller taillights fitted to '55 Mercs are shown on an entry-level $2218 Custom two-door sedan. **4-5.** Mercury's top four-door sedan was the $2685 Montclair.

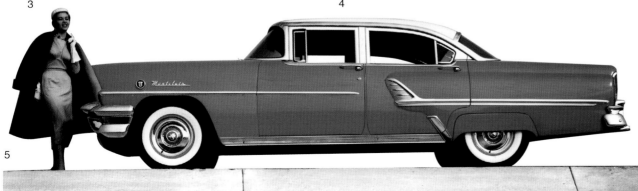

5

SCORECARD		1955
MAKE	TOTAL PRODUCTION	RANK
FORD	1,451,157 ▲	2nd ▼
LINCOLN	27,222 ▼	16th ▼
MERCURY	329,808 ▲	7th ●

1. Like most makes that were redesigned for 1955, Fords received only a mild facelift for '56. Sales of the glass-topped Fairlane Crown Victoria were down by two-thirds to a mere 603, perhaps due to their reputation for being mobile ovens. **2.** Ford heavily promoted its Y-Block V-8 (introduced for '54), though many of its cars were sold with the standard 223-cubic-inch six. For 1956, a 312-cid version of the V-8 was added to the carryover 272 and 292, with horsepower outputs now ranging from 173 to 215. Shown front and center in this ad is a Fairlane Victoria hardtop coupe. For 1956, it gained a four-door hardtop sibling, Ford's first hardtop sedan. **3-4.** Ever since station wagons went to all-steel construction in the early 1950s, sales had taken off: In Ford's case, they had increased ninefold since the beginning of the decade. Ford wagons made up their own series and were offered in a variety of styles and trim levels, including two-doors, four-doors, and the wood-grained Country Squire. For 1956, prices ranged from $2185 to $2533.

1

3

2

4

1

1. Thunderbirds got minor revisions for 1956. Most noticeable was a trunk-mounted spare tire, commonly called a "continental kit." Also, the optional hardtop gained its famous portholes, and front-fender vents were added just forward of the doors. Optional was Ford's new 312-cubic-inch V-8 with up to 225 horsepower. **2-4.** Lincoln was all new for 1956, being longer, lower, and wider. It also got 60 more horsepower, now 285, courtesy of an enlarged 368-cubic-inch V-8. Capri was now the entry model, Premiere the new top-line series. A Premiere four-door sedan went for $4601, a convertible for $4747.

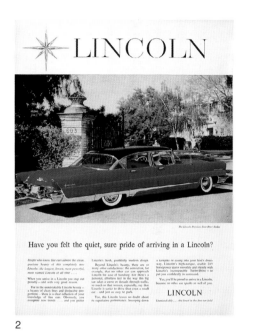

2

3

4

1

An experience awaits you—the excitement of being conservative

We think you will readily agree that the simple, straightforward lines of the new Continental *Mark II* are almost formal in their quiet elegance. To this extent, it is a conservative motor car. But observe how long and low and truly exciting a conservative car can be! It is an excitement you can actually sense—in owning it, and driving it and knowing that it is your own personal possession.

And always there will be the inner satisfaction of knowing that in the creation of the Continental *Mark II*, neither time nor craftsmanship have been stinted to make it as fine a motor car as America has yet known.

Continental
Mark II

Continental Division • Ford Motor Company

2

3

1-3. Added to the Ford Motor Company line for 1956 was the ultraluxury Continental Mark II. Offered only as a two-door coupe, it cost nearly $10,000—double that of a Lincoln. Inspired by the beautiful, low-slung, high-priced Lincoln Continentals of the '40s, it was likewise aimed at very discriminating (read "rich") buyers who appreciated distinctive styling, understated luxury, and exclusivity. And exclusive it was: Just 2556 were built for debut '56. Beneath the lengthy hood sat Lincoln's 285-horsepower 368-cubic-inch V-8. Ad writers took a rather unusual approach but perhaps knew their prospective buyers well, luring them with "the excitement of being conservative."

1. New to the Mercury line for 1956 was a four-door hardtop body style shared with Ford. Also added was a new entry-level series called Medalist. The four-door hardtop shown in the foreground is a top-line $2835 Montclair, but it was also offered in the other three Mercury trim levels: Medalist, Custom, and Monterey. 2. Mercury styling didn't change much for 1956, though the cars did get a revised front bumper and altered side trim. This $2712 Custom convertible sports the optional continental kit, which moved the spare tire to the back bumper. 3. The least expensive '56 Mercury, a $2254 Medalist two-door sedan, shows off the limited chrome trim applied to this new entry-level series. 4. A Custom two-door sedan cost about $100 more than its "stripped" Medalist counterpart, but looked classier thanks to its extra chrome trim. 5. Though the station wagon body was shared with Ford, Mercury's was mounted on a longer wheelbase. The taillights on Merc wagons were unique to this body style, as they had to fit the same outline as those on the Ford version. This Custom listed for $2722 in six-passenger form, $2819 outfitted for eight passengers.

SCORECARD		1956
MAKE	TOTAL PRODUCTION	RANK
CONTINENTAL	2,556	19th
FORD	1,408,478 ▼	2nd ●
LINCOLN	50,322 ▲	14th ▲
MERCURY	327,943 ▼	7th ●

1

2

3

1-3. Ford's advertising encouraged buyers to pick up "two fine Fords for the price of one fine car." This ad shows a family that took the bait, allowing "the men" to go fishing in a $2451 Ford Country Sedan station wagon, while "she's free as the breeze" in a flashy $2281 Fairlane 500 coupe. Maybe the strategy worked: In 1957, Ford beat Chevrolet in the production race, a feat it would manage only twice during the decade. **4.** Of course, some of that success may have been attributable to the fact the completely restyled '57 Ford was going up against a merely facelifted Chevy. A glamorous Fairlane 500 Sunliner convertible shows off Ford's sleek new lines that incorporated pronounced tailfins. It could have been yours for $2505. Another $437 would have bought Ford's new Skyliner convertible with its retractable hardtop. The top Ford engine remained a 312-cubic-inch V-8, now with 245 horsepower, up 30 from '56. **5.** Speaking of sleek new lines, the Thunderbird was also updated for 1957, with similar "blade" tailfins topping a longer rear deck. Front ends wore a cleaner grille, and the combination resulted in what was perhaps the best-looking of the two-seat T-Birds—and also the last. Horsepower of the 312-cid V-8 rose to as much as 285, with a supercharged version weighing in at a rousing 340. **6.** Ford also introduced the Ranchero for 1957, basically a two-door station wagon with the rear cargo area replaced by a pickup bed. This concept resulted in what the ad called "the sleekest pickup ever to pack a load," and would be copied two years later by Chevy's El Camino.

4

5

6

1

2

3

1. The limited-edition $10,000 Continental Mark II became even more limited for 1957, as only 444 copies were sold—down from 2556 the year before. Though the name would live on, 1957 would be the final year for this classic design. 2. Lincoln got a fresh face for 1957, though it differed little except for new stacked quad headlights. Prices rose significantly, the top-line Premiere convertible now commanding $5381. 3. Lincoln tailfins grew up and out for '57, becoming much more prominent. Also more prominent was the price of this Premiere two-door hardtop, which now stood at $5149. 4. Few cars changed more drastically for '57 than the redesigned Mercury. Heavy "eyebrows" over quad headlights distinguished the front, while the rear hosted channeled tailfins culminating in canted, U-shaped taillights. The cars looked far larger than their predecessors, and they were: Wheelbase was up by three inches on all versions. Model names were shuffled, too. Monterey was now the cheapest, followed by Montclair and the new Turnpike Cruiser. Prices ranged from $2576 to $4103. 5-6. Wagons now had their own series, and offered hardtop versions with two or four doors and prices from $2903 to $3677.

4

5

6

1

2

1-2. Newly installed at the top of the 1957 Mercury line was the chrome-bedecked Turnpike Cruiser. It was offered in only three body styles: convertible and two- or four-door hardtop. Hardtops featured a power-retractable reverse-slant rear window not shared with any other Mercury that year. Standard on the 'Cruiser was a new 290-horsepower 368-cubic-inch V-8, which was optional on other Mercs in place of a 255-horse 312. This Turnpike Cruiser two-door hardtop cost a princely $3758. **3.** A Turnpike Cruiser convertible—complete with spare tire continental kit in back—paced the 1957 running of the Indianapolis 500.

3

SCORECARD		1957
MAKE	TOTAL PRODUCTION	RANK
CONTINENTAL	444 ▲	19th ●
FORD	1,676,449 ▲	1st ▲
LINCOLN	41,123 ▼	14th ●
MERCURY	286,163 ▼	8th ▼

DRAMATIC EDSEL STYLING leads the way
—in distinction, in beauty, in value!

Last August, the photograph above could not have been taken. The Edsel car was still a secret then. But in one short year, Edsel's outstanding design has become as familiar as it is distinctive. In fact, you can recognize the classic Edsel lines much faster, much farther away, than you can any other car in America! This extra value in advanced styling accounts for the many more Edsels you've been seeing on the road lately.
And proud new Edsel owners are getting plenty of extra value inside their

cars, too—the ease of Teletouch Drive, the power and economy of the all-new engines, the convenience of self-adjusting brakes, the comfort of contour seats. And the satisfaction of having made a great buy. For there's less than fifty dollars difference between the magnificent Edsel and V-8's of the major low-priced makes.
Why not see your Edsel Dealer this week for sure!

EDSEL DIVISION • FORD MOTOR COMPANY

Less than fifty dollars between Edsel and V-8's of the major low-priced makes

1

Four-door hardtops *Two-door hardtops* *Station wagons* *Two- and four-door sedans*

Edsel Citation   Edsel Citation   Edsel Bermuda 9-passenger four-door   Edsel Ranger four-door
Edsel Corsair   Edsel Corsair   Edsel Bermuda 6-passenger four-door   Edsel Ranger two-door
Edsel Pacer   Edsel Pacer   Edsel Villager 9-passenger four-door   Edsel Pacer four-door
Edsel Ranger   Edsel Ranger   Edsel Villager 6-passenger four-door

Convertibles

Edsel Citation   Edsel Pacer   Edsel Roundup 6-passenger two-door

In any Edsel, you will have a matchless car. There are many things that make the Edsel different from any other car you have ever driven. What does an Edsel cost? Prices range from just above the lowest to just below the highest. You can afford an Edsel.

See Bing Crosby and Frank Sinatra star in The Edsel Show— live, on CBS-TV, Sunday, October 13.

EDSEL

New member of the Ford family of fine cars

2

1-4. An attempt to bridge the growing price gap between Ford and Mercury resulted in the 1958 introduction of the infamous Edsel. Named after Henry Ford II's older brother, who met an untimely death in 1943, none at the time could have known that "Edsel" would later become a synonym for "failure." But a failure it most certainly was, though not necessarily at first. In fact, it was in many ways a fine automobile—a fine automobile killed by a grille that would have looked more at home in the '30s. Oddly, the rear view was modern and attractive, with rear-fender coves and thin horizontal taillights. It wasn't until buyers saw a grille that looked as though it had been caught sucking a lemon that they turned away. But it didn't turn them *all* away, at least not in the beginning. Offered in a vast array of body styles and trim variations, more than 63,000 Edsels were sold that first year, which, though far below expectations, wasn't a horrible showing.

DRAMATIC EDSEL STYLING leads the way
—worth more now and in the years ahead

This is the fresh new beauty that broke away from the humdrum, look-alike crowd to offer real styling distinction. A distinction that's worth more when you buy it, worth more when you really trade it in. That's why you've been seeing a steady increase in new Edsels on the road lately! This magnificent new car stands out for its advanced new features, too—exclusive Teletouch Drive that puts the shift buttons on the

steering-wheel hub—right in front of you; high-economy new V-8 engines (up to 345 hp); self-adjusting brakes; and contour seats that give you luxurious driving comfort. Why settle for less? Especially when there isn't even fifty dollars difference between Edsel and the Low-Priced Three*! See your Edsel Dealer this week.

EDSEL DIVISION • FORD MOTOR COMPANY

Less than fifty dollars difference between Edsel and V-8's in the Low-Priced Three

3

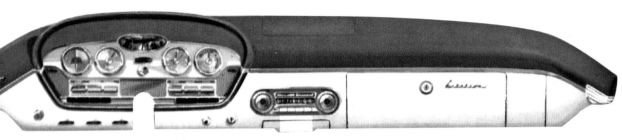

4

1

4

2

3

5

6

1. Edsels were offered in four series on two wheelbases: The shorter was shared with some Ford models, the longer was close to Mercury dimensions. The latter held the Corsair and top-line Citation, which were powered by a 345-horsepower 410-cubic-inch V-8. Shown is a $3535 Citation two-door hardtop, which carried a Mercury-like roofline. **2.** Ranger and Pacer rode the shorter Edsel chassis and got a 303-hp 361-cid V-8. This $2805 Pacer two-door hardtop sports a roofline similar to that used on Ford hardtops. **3.** Edsel offered Ranger and Pacer two- and four-door wagons that were based on those from sister division Ford. Edsel's wagon prices ranged from $2876 to $3247. **4-5.** Fords got a facelift for 1958, which brought quad headlights above a heavier grille and quad oval taillights. The top-line Fairlane 500 line offered two convertibles: the conventional Sunliner and the retractable-hardtop Skyliner. They were priced at $2650 and $3163, respectively. **6.** Also in the Fairlane family was the $2435 Victoria hardtop coupe. A hardtop sedan was offered as well, along with pillared versions of each.

1

2

3

4

5

1. Inside the '58 Ford brochure was information on the new 332- and 352-cubic-inch V-8s that supplanted the previous 312. Available horsepower ranged from 205 to a stout 300. **2.** Ford two- and four-door wagons again had their own series. Shown is the least expensive of them, the $2397 two-door Ranch Wagon. **3.** Thunderbird gained a new look and a rear seat in a radical 1958 redesign. Now a four-seater, the "Square Bird," as it became known, gained 11 inches in wheelbase and 800 lbs of weight. Convertible prices were up about $500 to $3929. **4-5.** A $3631 coupe was added to the line and promptly took the vast majority of sales—by a 16:1 margin. The only engine offered this year was the 300-horsepower 352-cubic-inch V-8 available in regular Fords.

1

1. If Mercury took the "Most Changed" crown for 1957, Lincoln likely earned it for '58. Where before Lincolns looked big and sleek, they now looked square and massive. Buyers evidently didn't like the change; prices were up only slightly, but sales dropped by 58 percent. Capri and Premiere series returned, both powered by a new 430-cubic-inch 375-horsepower V-8. A Premiere Landau hardtop sedan cost $5505. **2.** A change in philosophy made the once-exclusive Continental—now christened the Mark III—a gussied-up Lincoln at about $500 more. Offerings expanded to include a two-door hardtop, four-door hardtop and sedan, and this $6283 convertible, a body style no longer offered as a Lincoln. Though it watered down the Continental name, sales increased 28-fold. **3.** A Continental Mark III convertible faces the lineup offered at Lincoln-Mercury dealers for 1958.

2

3

1. Mercury styling was revised for 1958, but the biggest news was under the hood: Optional was Lincoln's 430-cubic-inch V-8—the largest engine sold in America—with up to 400 horsepower. Also new was a pushbutton transmission selector. This Montclair Turnpike Cruiser coupe cost $3498. **2.** Hardtop wagons were in their sophomore year, priced from $3035 to $3775. **3.** The new top-line Mercury for '58 was the Park Lane, which rode a longer wheelbase than other models. A four-door-hardtop version cost $3944.

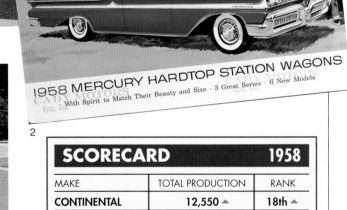

1958 MERCURY HARDTOP STATION WAGONS
With Spirit to Match Their Beauty and Size · 3 Great Series · 6 New Models

SCORECARD		1958
MAKE	TOTAL PRODUCTION	RANK
CONTINENTAL	12,550 ▲	18th ▲
EDSEL	63,110	12th
FORD	987,945 ▼	2nd ▼
LINCOLN	17,134 ▼	15th ▼
MERCURY	153,271 ▼	8th ●

1

2

3

4

1. In an effort to jump-start sales, Edsels received a number of changes for 1959. Among them was a new grille, which was a good thing, but it still incorporated the offensive "horse collar," which was not. The line was trimmed to just Ranger and Corsair, both now on the same wheelbase. The most expensive Edsel was this Corsair convertible, at $3072. **2.** Ads claimed Edsels now made more sense, partially due to a newly standard six-cylinder engine, which had not been previously offered. V-8s of 292, 332, and 361 cid were available that provided from 200 to 303 horsepower, but 1958's big 410-cid V-8 was dropped—something that also per- haps "made more sense." **3.** Edsel's tail treatment was altered as well, as shown on the make's cheapest model, the $2629 Ranger two-door sedan. **4.** Station wagons became their own series for 1959, and as before, shared bodies with their Ford counterparts. Just one model was offered: the $2989 Villager, with six- or optional nine-passenger seating. All these 1959 changes didn't help, as sales fell by nearly 30 percent, sounding the Edsel's death knell. A handful of restyled 1960 models were sold before the poor Edsel was branded a failure and resigned to automotive history.

1

2

1. Thunderbirds saw only minor trim changes for 1959, though newly optional was Lincoln's big 430-cubic-inch V-8 with 350 horsepower. **2-3.** Added for 1959 was the top-line Galaxie. Closed models, such as this $2582 four-door sedan, featured Thunderbird-like squared rear roof pillars. The top engine remained a 300-hp 352-cid V-8. **4.** Galaxie included Ford's only convertibles, the conventional Sunliner and the retractable-hardtop Skyliner (shown). **5.** Station wagons continued as a separate series, topped by the woodgrained $2958 Country Squire. For the most part, Ford would spend the next four decades playing second fiddle to Chevrolet, as it continues to do today.

3

4

5

1

1-2. Continental lost its separate-marque status for 1959, being folded into the Lincoln brand as the top-line model. Now called the Mark IV, it received only minor styling changes, including an altered side-cove treatment and rectangular taillights. The four-door hardtop listed for $6845, about $1250 to $1750 more than comparable Premiere and base-model siblings. **3.** Added to the Continental line was this $9208 formal sedan, with distinctive vinyl-covered top and thick rear roof pillars. Lincoln left the decade as it entered it, in second place behind Cadillac in the American luxury-car sweepstakes.

2

3

1

2

1-2. Mercury's tailfin coves were extended forward for 1959, and the taillights they held were altered a bit. The grille was also restyled. Station wagons came in two- and four-door versions, with prices ranging from $3145 to $3932. **3.** Medalist was dropped for 1959, leaving Monterey, Montclair, and top-line Park Lane. This Montclair Cruiser four-door hardtop went for $3437. **4.** The available 430-cubic-inch V-8 was detuned to "only" 345 horsepower for 1959, and offered only in Park Lanes, like this $4031 Cruiser four-door hardtop. With the demise of Edsel in mid 1960, Mercury became Ford Motor Company's sole midprice line. It kept its distinct identity into the 1970s, during which the cars became little more than gussied-up Fords.

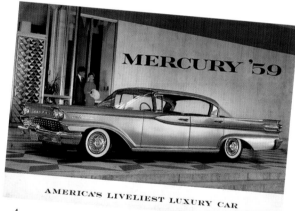

MERCURY '59

AMERICA'S LIVELIEST LUXURY CAR

4

3

SCORECARD		1959
MAKE	TOTAL PRODUCTION	RANK
EDSEL	44,891 ▼	14th ▼
FORD	1,450,953 ▲	2nd ●
LINCOLN	26,906 ▲	15th ●
MERCURY	149,987 ▼	9th ▼

Monolithic General Motors was incorporated in 1908 by hard-charging William C. Durant, who brought together Buick (founded 1903), Oldsmobile (1897), and soon thereafter, Cadillac (1902) to form what would eventually become the world's largest corporation. Though Durant was ousted two years later, he went on to start Chevrolet in 1911, which grew quickly and was itself brought into the GM fold by 1918—along with Durant, who regained power. Pontiac was added along with four other "companion" makes during the 1920s, and was the only one of the quintet to survive past 1940. By that time, Durant was gone (again), and the helm was now in the hands of Alfred P. Sloan, who established the successful "price ladder" that drove GM to greatness and became the model for other car companies—most notably Chrysler Corp., and to a lesser extent, Ford Motor Company.

As GM entered the 1950s, Chevrolet was the best-selling car in the land, with Buick, Pontiac, and Oldsmobile all in the top six. Cadillac was down in 14th place, but was by far the most popular luxury make. Each had its own niche during the era: Chevrolet was the price leader, Pontiac enjoyed a reputation for reliability, Oldsmobile was known for performance and engineering, Buick was the "doctor's car," and Cadillac the "Standard of the World." By the end of the decade, Chevrolet was still in first place, with all its siblings in the top ten. In all, the Fifties were very, very good to General Motors.

1

2

1. Buick's 1949 redesign included the first of the marque's signature "portholes" on the front fenders. The low-line Special and midline Super (shown in sedan form) got three on each side. A 1950 update brought a massive, bucktooth grille and a kick-up in the rear fender line. All models were powered by one of Buick's famous straight-eight engines. Spanning a price range of $1803 to $1983, the Special had a 248-cubic-inch version with 115/120 horsepower. Supers cost about $200 more and had a 263 with 124/128 hp. **2.** Buick's top-line $2633 Roadmaster Riviera hardtop coupe got four portholes and a 322-cid eight with 152 hp.

1. Cadillac's 1948 redesign included its trademark tailfins, the first of what became a Fifties phenomenon. The next year brought its equally revolutionary short-stroke overhead-valve V-8. Sized at 331 cubic inches, it produced a then-impressive 160 horsepower. It would eventually put out as much as 270. The Series 61 sedan was priced at $2866.

2. New for 1950 Cadillacs was a one-piece windshield, as shown on this $2761 hardtop coupe representing the Series 61 line—the least expensive Cadillacs offered. The flashier Series 62s cost about $200 more. Also offered was a lone Series Sixty Special sedan at $3828, and a line of low-production long-wheelbase Series 75 models priced at a whopping $4650 to $5170.

3. Chevrolet represented the opposite end of the GM price spectrum, though this snazzy red Styleline Deluxe convertible hardly looks the part. At $1847 it was the most expensive 1950 Chevy, with lesser models starting as low as $1329.

4. This $1529 Styleline Deluxe sedan was Chevy's most popular car. It was available with the newly introduced two-speed Powerglide transmission, making it the only one of the "low-priced three" (Chevy, Ford, and Plymouth) to offer an automatic—a big advantage that was enough to vault Chevy into first place in the sales race: At nearly 1.5 million sold, it outgunned rival Ford by almost 300,000 units. Standard was a 92-hp 216-cid six, but Powerglide cars got a 105-hp 235.

5. Chevy's new Bel Air was America's first low-price hardtop coupe at $1741. It was available in a variety of two-tone color schemes.

1

2

3

4

5

1

2

5

3

4

6

1. Oldsmobile introduced America's first fully automatic transmission for 1940. Hydra-Matic was a stunning engineering coup, and was eventually used not only by other GM makes but by other car companies as well. With the introduction of its short-stroke, overhead-valve Rocket V-8 engine for 1949, Oldsmobile became not only a technology leader, but also a race-winner. The 303-cubic-inch 135-horsepower Rocket powered many an Olds 88 to victory on the stock-car tracks. It was also used in Oldsmobile's larger—and heavier—98. The bottom-line Olds 76 carried a 237-cid six making 105 hp. Oldsmobile prices ranged from $1719 to $2772. This sporty 88 Deluxe sedan went for $2056. **2.** Perhaps more fitting of the "sporty" label was this racy 88 convertible. **3.** Olds offered both notchback and fastback sedans for 1950, but it would be the fastback's final year. Shown is an 88 two-door club sedan. **4.** To separate them from "lesser" Oldsmobiles, top-line 98s got peaked rear fenders hosting round taillights. **5.** Pontiacs were powered by straight sixes and eights of 239/268 cid and 90 to 113 hp. They were priced from $1673 to the $2190 of this Chieftain Eight convertible, placing them between Chevrolet and Oldsmobile on the corporate ladder. Pontiacs were known for their chrome hood and trunklid strakes and gold chief's-head hood ornaments. **6.** Two-door hardtops appeared for 1950, introducing the Catalina name.

SCORECARD		1950
MAKE	TOTAL PRODUCTION	RANK
BUICK	667,826 ▲	3rd ▲
CADILLAC	103,857 ▲	14th ▲
CHEVROLET	1,498,590 ▲	1st ▲
OLDSMOBILE	407,889 ▲	6th ▲
PONTIAC	466,429 ▲	5th ●

1

1. Buick's former bucktooth grille was tamed a bit for 1951. The three front-fender portholes (officially called VentiPorts) identify this convertible as either a Special or Super, as the top-line Roadmaster had four. For those gripped by suspense, it's the $2728 Super. Note the "Dynaflow" badge on the rear fender. Dynaflow was Buick's automatic transmission. Its torque converter made it very smooth in operation, but because of its intended slippage (and resulting hindrance to performance) some detractors derided it as the "Dynaslush." **2-3.** Cadillacs changed little in appearance for 1951, though all now came standard with Hydra-Matic, GM's (originally Oldsmobile's) four-speed automatic transmission. The stately Series 62 is represented by a $3987 convertible and $3843 Coupe de Ville hardtop.

2

3

1. Chevys got a mild "taillift" for 1951, with rear fenders that were squared off at the trailing edge. By this time, all GM makes except Chevrolet had dropped their four-door fastbacks due to slowing sales, and Chevy's would join them after this year. A two-door version would hold out a year longer. Fastbacks were called Fleetlines, and are represented here by a very rare $1594 Fleetline Special four-door. **2.** Styleline Special was the Fleetline's notchback counterpart, which sold for the same price but was far more popular. This Styleline Special two-door sedan went for $1540. **3.** Pontiac celebrated its 25th anniversary in 1951 with a very mild facelift. **4.** Oldsmobile dropped its six-cylinder engine for '51, so all models carried a Rocket V-8. Added that year was the midline Super 88, shown here in $2328 four-door sedan guise. **5.** The big Olds 98 again featured a unique taillight and side-trim treatment. Shown is the Holiday hardtop coupe.

1

3

2

4

5

SCORECARD		1951
MAKE	TOTAL PRODUCTION	RANK
BUICK	592,511 ▼	4th ▼
CADILLAC	110,340 ▲	14th ●
CHEVROLET	1,229,986 ▼	1st ●
OLDSMOBILE	285,615 ▼	8th ▼
PONTIAC	370,159 ▼	5th ●

1

2

3

4

5

1. Buicks gained tiny chrome tailfins and revised side trim for 1952, but were otherwise little-changed. A Super convertible was $2869. **2.** Buick's "woody" wagons saw very limited production during these years, mostly due to their high price. This Super wagon cost $3296 and sold just 1641 copies. In Roadmaster form, it went for the princely sum of $3977—making it far and away Buick's most expensive car—and attracted only 359 well-heeled buyers. **3.** Cadillac celebrated its golden anniversary in 1952 still entrenched as the country's best-selling luxury make, despite negligible styling changes. Sales may have gotten a little boost, however, thanks to a power increase that bumped the 331-cubic-inch V-8 from 160 horses to 190—making it the most potent engine in the industry. Another "boost" came in the form of newly available power steering, a feature shared with Oldsmobile. Also new was Autronic Eye, which automatically dimmed the high beams when it detected the headlights of oncoming traffic. The "low-line" Series 61 was dropped for 1952, leaving the Series 62 as the entry-level model. A Series 62 Coupe de Ville hardtop could be parked in your driveway for $4013. **4-5.** A Series 62 convertible cost $150 more—a small price to pay for what many believed was the ultimate in open-air motoring.

1

2

1. Chevrolets were little-changed for 1952, yet easily remained number one in U.S. sales. One of the more popular models was this $1761 Styleline Deluxe sedan. **2.** Considering Chevy's low-price status, the sporty but comparatively expensive Bel Air two-door hardtop sold an impressive 74,000 copies at $2006. **3.** A $2673 Super 88 Holiday hardtop coupe could be optioned with newly available power steering and Autronic Eye automatic headlight dimmer, both shared with Cadillac. **4.** Super 88s (shown in four-door-sedan form) and 98s (now spelled out as "Ninety-Eight") enjoyed a 25-horsepower boost for '52, bringing the total to 160. **5.** Pontiacs again saw few changes for the new year, yet retained their stranglehold on the number-five sales position. A 122-hp Chieftain Eight Super Deluxe Catalina hardtop coupe cost a lot of breath to say, but only $2446 to buy.

3

4

5

108

SCORECARD		1952
MAKE	TOTAL PRODUCTION	RANK
BUICK	367,760 ▼	4th ●
CADILLAC	90,259 ▼	11th ▲
CHEVROLET	818,142 ▼	1st ●
OLDSMOBILE	213,490 ▼	6th ▲
PONTIAC	271,373 ▼	5th ●

1

2

3

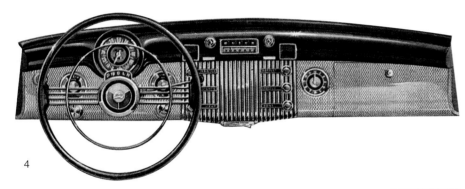

4

1-2. Buicks received a number of changes for 1953 to celebrate the division's 50th anniversary. Freshened styling was punctuated by twin bullet taillights, and while entry-level Specials retained a 263-cubic-inch inline eight, Supers and Roadmasters got a new 322-cid overhead-valve V-8 making 188 horsepower. The outrageously priced woody wagons were in their final year; subsequent wagons would be less expensive all-steel versions. **3-4.** A Roadmaster convertible tipped the price scale at $3506. **5-6.** GM introduced a striking trio of specialty convertibles for 1953. Buick's was the stunning—and stunningly expensive—Skylark. At $5000, it cost $1500 more than a similar Roadmaster. It featured a cut-down windshield and lower silhouette, along with rounded wheelwell cutouts and standard wire wheels. Only 1690 were built, one reason these gorgeous cars are such coveted classics today.

5

6

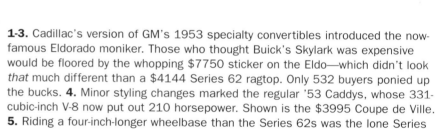

1-3. Cadillac's version of GM's 1953 specialty convertibles introduced the now-famous Eldorado moniker. Those who thought Buick's Skylark was expensive would be floored by the whopping $7750 sticker on the Eldo—which didn't look *that* much different than a $4144 Series 62 ragtop. Only 532 buyers ponied up the bucks. **4.** Minor styling changes marked the regular '53 Caddys, whose 331-cubic-inch V-8 now put out 210 horsepower. Shown is the $3995 Coupe de Ville. **5.** Riding a four-inch-longer wheelbase than the Series 62s was the lone Series Sixty Special four-door sedan priced at $4305.

1

2

3

1-3. What started as a 1953 Motorama show car went on sale a scant six months later as the legendary Corvette. Unfortunately, its mechanical components couldn't support the promise made by its racy, two-seat fiberglass body. Beneath the hood was Chevy's aging 235-cubic-inch six, and though boosted from 115 horsepower to 150 for this application, it was backed by the company's Powerglide two-speed automatic transmission—a scourge to sports-car purists, who preferred manual transmissions. Priced at a stiff $3515, production was limited to just 315 units—all of them Polo White with red interiors. **4-5.** More palatable to 1953 ragtop fans was the top-line Bel Air convertible at $2175. **6.** Considering Chevy was a low-price make, it's surprising the flashy $1874 Bel Air sedan sold nearly a quarter-million copies.

4

5

6

1

2

OLDSMOBILE'S FABULOUS NEW Fiesta

A Custom Classic with a festive flair! It's Fiesta—
the merriest, most magnificent Oldsmobile ever
built—with low-sweeping silhouette, panoramic
windshield . . . a galaxy of glamour features! For
the discriminating motorist—it's the sports car supreme!

3

1-3. Rounding out the trio of GM's 1953 specialty convertibles was Oldsmobile's flashy Fiesta. It carried unique "spinner" wheelcovers, knockoffs of which became widely favored by customizers. Less popular was the car itself: at a lofty $5717, it fell between the Buick Skylark and Cadillac Eldorado in price, and didn't match the sales of either. Just 458 found buyers. **4.** Oldsmobiles earned some styling changes for 1953. They were most noticeable on the 88, which now had a similar tail treatment to the Ninety-Eight. **5.** This Ninety-Eight Holiday coupe wears fashionable wire wheels.

4

5

2

3

1. Dependability may have been a solid selling point in 1953, but it was a long way from the performance image Pontiac would push later in the decade. **2.** A rare hauler is this sedan delivery, with its blanked-out rear side windows. **3.** Pontiacs were treated to a longer wheelbase and major reskin for '53. A one-piece windshield appeared, along with kicked-up rear fenders. **4-5.** Extra chrome was added as well, as evidenced by this $2446 Chieftain Eight Custom Catalina hardtop. Eights only cost about $75 more than comparable Sixes, and for good reason: When GM's Hydra-Matic automatic transmission was ordered—which was about 75 percent of the time—the six-cylinder engine now put out 118 horsepower, while the eight remained at 122. Newly optional for '53 was power steering.

1

4

5

SCORECARD		1953
MAKE	TOTAL PRODUCTION	RANK
BUICK	486,812 ▲	4th ●
CADILLAC	109,651 ▲	13th ▼
CHEVROLET	1,346,475 ▲	1st ●
OLDSMOBILE	334,462 ▲	6th ●
PONTIAC	418,619 ▲	5th ●

1

2

4

1-3. The exotic Skylark specialty convertible returned for 1954, but this time, it was just a little less special. It was also a little less expensive: $4483 versus the $5000 asked for the '53 version. It was essentially a standard convertible with shaved portholes, sloping trunklid, and unique taillights. **4.** The Skylark's resemblance to a $2964 Super convertible is obvious. All Buicks got larger, "squarer" bodies for '54, along with wraparound windshields. **5.** The surviving straight-eight engine in the Special was axed, replaced by a 264-cubic-inch 150-horsepower version of the upper models' 322-cid V-8, which added ponies for '54: up to 200 in the top-line Roadmaster. That engine was also offered in a new "hot rod" Buick (seemingly a contradiction) called the Century. Actually, the name—and the concept—weren't new. Before World War II, a Century carried Buick's biggest engine in a midsize body, and was named for its ability to hit 100 mph right off the showroom floor. For 1954, it was offered in coupe, convertible, and sedan forms, along with this unlikely station wagon, which listed for $3470.

3

5

1

2

3

1-2. Like Buicks, Cadillacs got squared-up bodies for 1954 along with a new front-end treatment. Wheelbases grew by three inches, and the 331 V-8 produced 20 more horsepower, now 230. By far the most popular Cadillac was this $3933 Series 62 sedan. **3.** Like its Buick Skylark counterpart, the specialty Eldorado convertible returned for '54, also ending up a closer relation to other cars in the line. This was reflected in a price cut of more than $2000, putting it at a "mere" $5738. A regular Series 62 convertible cost $1300 less. **4-5.** Chevys got a mild facelift for 1954, and their 235-cubic-inch six gained 10 horsepower, for a top rating of 125. **6.** Corvette color choices quadrupled with the addition of blue, red, and black to the carry-over white. Production increased more than tenfold to 3640.

4

5

6

1

2

3

4

1-2. Joining the "squarer body brigade" led by Buick and Cadillac, 1954 Oldsmobiles boasted a much sleeker, more modern look. All models gained two inches in wheelbase, and engine size increased from 303 cubic inches to 324. That brought 185 horses to the Super 88 corral. A Holiday coupe cost $2688, a convertible, $2868. **3.** Replacing the slow-selling Fiesta specialty convertible was the new Starfire, likewise offered only in ragtop form. It was essentially the topline Ninety-Eight convertible with a fancy name and special trim. It was easily distinguishable by its "spectacular sweepcut rear fenders"—by which was meant the wheelwell cutouts. It listed for $3276, about the same as the previous Ninety-Eight convertible, and oceans less than the $5717 Fiesta. **4.** Sharing the Starfire's spectacular fenders was the $2826 Ninety-Eight Holiday hardtop coupe. Ninety-Eight sedans didn't get the feature.

1

2

4

3

5

1-2. A new top-line Pontiac arrived for 1954 with a longer wheelbase than other models. Called the Star Chief, it featured extended rear quarter panels and unique trim. Prices ran about $100 more than comparable Chieftain Eights. This Star Chief Catalina hardtop listed for $2557. **3-4.** Since Pontiacs received only minor trim changes for 1954, they looked a bit dated next to their rebodied Buick and Olds counterparts. They also cost a bit more: In two-door hardtop form, this $2458 Chieftain Eight Custom Catalina was $153 more than a Buick Special, $9 more than an Olds 88. **5.** A Chieftain Six two-door sedan was the cheapest Pontiac at $1968.

SCORECARD		**1954**
MAKE	TOTAL PRODUCTION	RANK
BUICK	442,903 ▼	4th ●
CADILLAC	96,680 ▼	10th ▲
CHEVROLET	1,143,561 ▼	2nd ▼
OLDSMOBILE	354,001 ▲	5th ▲
PONTIAC	287,744 ▼	6th ▼

1

2

3

1-2. Buicks were redesigned for 1955, and wore their revised lines particularly well. Front ends took on a Cadillac character with a massive chrome grille and bumper accented with bullet-shaped bumper extensions. Augmenting the returning two- and four-door sedans, two-door hardtops and convertibles, and four-door wagons was a new four-door hardtop without center roof pillars. Referred to as the Riviera hardtop sedan, it's shown here in entry-level Special trim, attractively priced at $2409 with a 188-horsepower 264-cubic-inch V-8. **3.** Centurys continued as the hot-rod Buick, hosting the larger 322-cid V-8 found in top-line Roadmasters in the shorter, lighter Special body. Horsepower of this engine was raised to 236 for 1955, making Century a potent pursuit vehicle. **4.** A "hauler" in every sense of the word was this $3175 Century station wagon.

4

1

2

3

4

1-2. While "everyday" Cadillacs continued into 1955 with few changes, the exotic Eldorado received a unique tail treatment that foreshadowed what its stablemates would get three years hence. At $6286, the Eldo remained staggeringly expensive. **3.** Those who blanched at the Eldorado's price could save nearly $1800 by picking a Series 62 convertible. **4.** The Series 62 four-door sedan retained its title as the most popular Cadillac, but wouldn't for much longer. All Caddys got a horsepower boost for 1955, setting the standard cars at 250, the Eldorado at 270.

CHEVROLET 1955

New Look! New Life (V8 OR 6)! New Everything!

1

1. Chevy's 1955 brochure exclaimed "New Everything!," and it wasn't an exaggeration. Besides the all-new look, the company released its first V-8 in 35 years: a short-stroke, overhead-valve wonder that would carry on in its basic form for more than four decades. Sized at 265 cubic inches, it produced as much as 180 horsepower. Still offered as the base engine was a 235-cid six. 2. On November 23, 1954, a special gold-trimmed '55 Bel Air became the 50-millionth General Motors car to roll off an assembly line. 3. Newly offered by Chevrolet was the two-door Nomad wagon, which would become among the most collectible of the '55 closed models. It was available only as a top-line Bel Air at $2472. 4. A $2206 Bel Air convertible is shown decked out with optional continental kit, which moved the spare tire to an enclosed case mounted on the rear bumper. A similar car paced the 1955 running of the Indy 500. 5. Corvette got a much-needed injection of power in the form of Chevy's new V-8, which offered 195 hp. Also available (finally) was a three-speed manual transmission. Yet sales sank to just 674—mostly due to Ford's new Thunderbird.

2

3

4

5

1

2

1. After being updated for 1954, Oldsmobile entered 1955 with relatively minor changes. This put it at a disadvantage against the rash of redesigned vehicles introduced that year, especially since it didn't get much help in the powertrain department: The top 324-cubic-inch Rocket V-8 gained a modest (for 1955) 18 horsepower, coming in at 202. Yet amazingly, Olds not only held its own, but advanced—from fifth place to fourth in industry sales. The Ninety-Eight Starfire convertible remained the most expensive Olds at $3276. **2.** Newly available for 1955 was a four-door hardtop, what Olds called a Holiday hardtop sedan. It was offered in all series—88, Super 88, and Ninety-Eight—and cost $186 to $307 more than a comparable four-door pillared sedan. That was quite a lot in 1955 dollars, yet the four-door hardtops sold very well. This Ninety-Eight Holiday hardtop sedan went for $3140. **3.** At the opposite end of the hardtop price spectrum was the 88 Holiday hardtop coupe at $2474. **4.** A plain-

Jane 88 two-door sedan—devoid of two-tone lower-body paint or whitewall tires—is a rare sight today. In 1955, it was Oldsmobile's entry-level model at $2297.

3

4

1

2

Pontiac creates an entirely new type of car combining Catalina smartness and station wagon utility

This completely new Star Chief from the originator of hardtop styling is easily the most versatile of motor cars. Appointed with traditional Catalina luxury, yet retaining all the spacious practicality of a station wagon, the Safari will serve you equally well as a smart town car, a wondrously comfortable touring companion, or a hard-working carrier. It is powered, of course, by the sensational Strato-Streak V-8 for performance as distinctive as its beauty. See it today—the price will delight you as much as the car!

THE PONTIAC *Safari*

5

6

1-4. Pontiacs took on a whole new look for 1955 yet retained many signature styling cues. Sleek side panels culminated in a kick-up at the rear, beneath which sat the traditional round taillights. Hoods wore the usual "silver streaks," though they now ran in two rows. Also new was the company's first V-8. The 287-cubic-inch overhead-valve Strato-Streak made 180 horsepower, or 200 with optional four-barrel carburetor. A Starchief Custom Catalina hardtop coupe listed at $2499. **5.** The ability to drop the top on your Star Chief cost an extra $192. **6.** Newly installed as Pontiac's most expensive car was the $2962 Custom Safari wagon. It mimicked Chevy's Nomad wagon in having two doors and semi-hardtop styling, but rode a longer wheelbase and cost $500 more.

3

4

SCORECARD		1955
MAKE	TOTAL PRODUCTION	RANK
BUICK	737,035 ▲	3rd ▲
CADILLAC	140,777 ▲	10th ●
CHEVROLET	1,704,667 ▲	1st ▲
OLDSMOBILE	583,179 ▲	4th ▲
PONTIAC	553,808 ▲	5th ▲

1

2

3

4

5

6

1. Buicks got minor front and rear styling updates for 1956 along with a few more ponies for the 322-cubic-inch V-8, now with up to 255 hp. Those seeking open-air enjoyment with Buick luxury could find it in the $2740 Special convertible. **2.** A top-line Roadmaster sedan listed for $3503. It was far outsold by its fancier four-door-hardtop sibling, which cost $189 more. **3.** Wagons were offered as entry-level 220-hp Specials (shown) or hot-rod 255-hp Centurys. They cost $2775 and $3256, respectively. **4.** Cadillacs didn't look much different for 1956, and that included the high-end $6556 Eldorado convertible, which added "Biarritz" to its name. It was joined by a two-door-hardtop version called the Eldorado Seville, which cost the same. **5.** A smaller-mesh grille was the biggest front-end change to the '56 Caddy. But behind the grille sat an enlarged V-8 that grew from 331 cubic inches to 365, bringing with it 285 horses in base form, 305 in the Eldorado. The stately $5047 Sixty Special sedan rode a four-inch-longer wheelbase than its Series 62 counterpart, which partially explains its near-$800 price premium. **6.** Tailfins wore flat tops for 1956, as shown on this $4624 Coupe de Ville. Joining it that year was a four-door hardtop called Sedan de Ville. Both names would continue to grace Cadillacs for decades to come.

1. Chevrolet picked up the pace for 1956 with a mild facelift and more power: up to 225 horses from the 265-cubic-inch V-8. Ads proclaimed "The Hot One's Even Hotter." And indeed it was. Zora Arkus-Duntov, renowned for his work with the Corvette, set an American Stock Sedan record in the grueling Pikes Peak Hill Climb. His time of 17 minutes, 24 seconds beat the old record by a resounding two minutes. The top V-8 could be ordered in any '56 Chevy, including this entry-level 150 two-door sedan, yours (at the time) for just $1826. **2.** At the opposite end of the two-door spectrum was the Bel Air Sport hardtop at $2176. **3.** Most popular of the '56 Chevys was the midline 210 Series. And the most popular 210 was the $1955 four-door sedan. **4.** Among "regular" Chevrolets, the $2608 two-door Nomad wagon still topped the price ladder for 1956. To many, its sporty good looks made it worth the $126 it cost over and above a comparable four-door Bel Air wagon. **5.** Chevy finally got on board the four-door hard-top train in '56 with the Sport hardtop sedan. Offered in 210 (shown) and fancier Bel Air trim, the hardtops cost $162 more than regular four-door pillared sedans. That put the 210 version at $2117, the Bel Air at $2230.

1

2

3

4

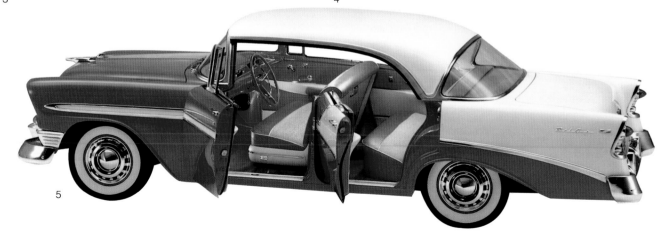

5

1

2

3

1-3. Corvette got a radical makeover for 1956 that likely spared its life. Not only did it look better, but the redesign brought expected features such as roll-up windows (the original had clumsy snap-in side curtains) and outside door handles (owners previously had to reach inside the car to open the latch). Newly optional were power windows, a power convertible top, and a detachable hardtop. Up to 225 horsepower was now offered, which didn't hurt, either. The price rose a bit to $3149, while sales rose fivefold to 3467. The Corvette's bodyside coves were a distinctive styling element that made the car instantly recognizable. They would last through the end of this styling generation in 1962. **4.** A large "loop" front bumper and revised side trim marked the 1956 Oldsmobiles, which otherwise hadn't changed much since '54. This was rather unusual for the time period, as annual styling changes were considered necessary to maintain sales. And indeed, Olds dropped back down to fifth in industry production. The line-topping Ninety-Eight Starfire convertible demanded $3740. **5.** Less demanding was the Super 88 Holiday hardtop coupe at $2808. **6.** Oldsmobile's V-8 remained at 324 cubic inches for '56, but power rose from 202 horsepower to 240 in the Super 88 and this Ninety-Eight Holiday four-door hardtop sedan.

4

5

6

1

2

3

4

1. Like Chevrolet, Pontiac belatedly added a four-door hardtop body style to its lineup for 1956. Shown is the top-line Star Chief version, which went for $2735. Other Star Chief body styles included the $2665 Custom Catalina hardtop coupe **(2)**, the $3129 Safari two-door wagon **(3)**, and $2857 convertible **(4)**. Lower-line models were called Chieftains. All carried a larger 316-cubic-inch V-8 rated from 192 horsepower to a rousing 285 with high compression and twin four-barrel carburetors. **5.** Four-door wagons shared rear fenders with Chevrolet wagons, and thus carried unique Chevy-shaped taillights. Offered only in the Chieftain series, this nine-passenger version cost $2653.

5

SCORECARD		1956
MAKE	TOTAL PRODUCTION	RANK
BUICK	635,158 ▼	3rd ●
CADILLAC	154,577 ▲	9th ▲
CHEVROLET	1,567,117 ▼	1st ●
OLDSMOBILE	485,458 ▼	5th ▼
PONTIAC	405,429 ▼	6th ▼

1

2

3

4

1. Buicks looked longer and lower for 1957, especially on the long-wheelbase chassis shared by the top-line Roadmaster (coupe shown) and midline Super. A larger 364-cubic-inch V-8 powered all Buicks that year. As had become tradition, the Roadmaster and the shorter, lighter, hot-rod Century got more power than other models: For 1957, that meant 300 horses vs. 250 for the Super and price-leading Special. Those figures were up by 45 and 30, respectively, over 1956. Buick prices ranged from $2596 for a Special two-door sedan to $4483 for the top Roadmaster four-door hardtop. **2.** A Century wasn't Buick's lowest-priced convertible, but it was certainly its fastest. At $3598, it cost $600 more than its Special counterpart, and about $500 less than a Roadmaster ragtop. **3.** The Century line also hosted the sporty new Caballero four-door hardtop wagon. It was Buick's best-selling wagon in '57, despite the fact its $3706 price made it by far the most expensive. **4.** These cowboys (and girls) seem to admire the room, comfort, power, and class afforded by a $3354 Century Riviera hardtop sedan.

2

Magnificent Beyond All Expectations!

When a new Cadillac car is imminent on the American motoring scene, it is usually expected that the car will be dramatically advanced . . . and that it will raise the world's standards of automotive excellence.

But no one, not even Cadillac owners themselves, was fully prepared for the beautiful new Cadillac pictured above. The brilliant creation literally contradicted the bolder hope.

But then, how could anyone have anticipated a motor car so beautiful to behold as this newest "car of cars"? Its graceful, flowing lines and its great majesty and elegance are simply without precedent in the annals of automotive design.

And how could anyone have foreseen a motor car of such rare luxury and comfort? Inside are fabrics and luxuries and appointments beyond anything ever offered before in a modern day motor car.

And how, to be sure, could anyone have predicted a motor car so brilliant in performance? Its magnificent new power and responsiveness and its extraordinary ease of ride and handling have no counterpart even in Cadillac's glorious past.

We suggest that you pay an early visit to our showroom for a personal inspection and demonstration of this new 1957 Cadillac.

Come with your hopes set high—and you'll still be very pleasantly surprised with this latest and greatest of Cadillacs!

Cadillac

YOUR CADILLAC DEALER

1

3

4

1. Cadillacs received a long-overdue redesign for 1957 that faithfully followed the "longer, lower, wider" mantra that prevailed during the decade—though it wasn't to the extreme depicted by the illustration in this ad. If the tail treatment looks familiar, it should: The high-end Eldorados had been wearing something very similar since '55.
2. Front ends changed dramatically as well, though were still recognizable as Cadillacs. Most prices rose about $400-$700, bringing this Coupe de Ville in at $5116. **3-4.** In order to retain a unique identity—and justify their higher prices—Eldorados again displayed distinctive rear styling, with sharklike fins protruding from a sloping decklid. The convertible retained its Biarritz surname, the coupe its Seville suffix. Added (but not shown here) was a Seville four-door hardtop. All these Eldos carried the same $7286 base price. **5.** If these Eldorados weren't sufficiently exclusive (read "expensive") for you, perhaps the new Eldorado Brougham would fill the bill—if indeed you could handle a bill that totaled a stratospheric $13,074. For that you got a specially built body with "suicide" rear doors, brushed stainless-steel roof, and quad headlights, along with an air-spring suspension and the virtual assurance you wouldn't see another car like yours on the road.

5

1

2

1. For 1957, Chevrolet introduced what would become one of the most iconic cars of the Fifties. Though actually just a facelift of the '56 (itself a facelift of the '55), the '57 Chevy was a landmark design that still looks good today. **2-3.** One of the highlights of the year was a fuel-injected version of Chevy's newly enlarged 283-cubic-inch V-8 that produced up to 283 horsepower—the revered "one horsepower per cubic inch." Chrysler had done it the year before with the Hemi-powered 300-B, but that was a high-priced car that cost twice as much as the average Chevy. The "fuelie" engine was available on all models, including this bare-bones 150 utility sedan that started at just $1885. **4.** The Nomad was back, looking better than ever at $2757.

5. One of the most popular '57 Chevys was the top-line $2290 Bel Air four-door sedan. **6.** Corvette looked little different for '57, but all engines gained power and a newly optional four-speed manual transmission made better use of it. A four-speed '57 fuelie—such as the one shown—was a formidable street car that was equally at home on a racetrack.

3

4

5

6

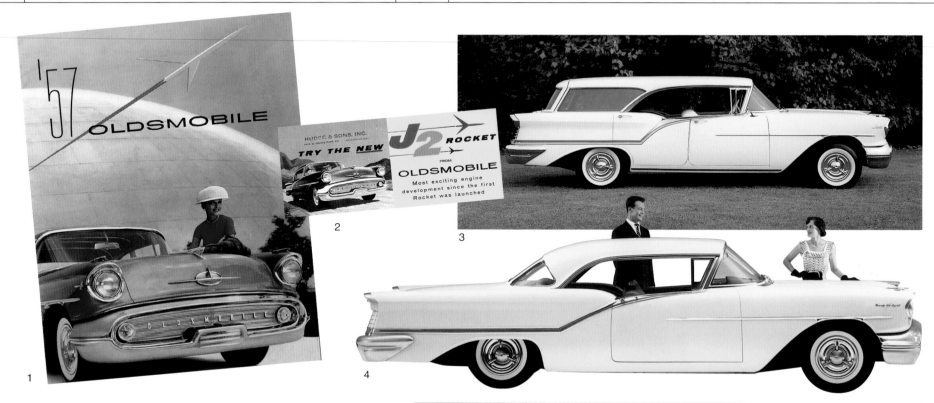

1-2. Having been outpaced in the horsepower race during 1956 by sibling rivals Buick and Pontiac, Oldsmobile made a gallant effort to catch up for '57 with increased displacement (up from 324 cubic inches to 371) and the potent J-2 engine option. Consisting of a trio of two-barrel carburetors, this setup raised horsepower from the standard 277 to an even 300, giving a J-2 Olds strong street performance. **3.** Not since 1950 had Olds offered station wagons, but they returned for '57 under the Fiesta moniker. Offered in 88 and Super 88 trim (both adding "Golden Rocket" as a prefix to their names for '57 in celebration of Oldsmobile's 60th anniversary), Fiestas were available in both pillared and pillarless versions. Shown is the $3541 Golden Rocket Super 88 Fiesta hardtop wagon. **4.** Not to be outdone, the Ninety-Eight became the Starfire Ninety-Eight, shown here as the $3937 Holiday hardtop coupe. **5.** Convertibles were offered in all three series, this being the Super 88—er, Golden Rocket Super 88—ragtop, which listed for $3447.

1

2

3

4

1-2. It was during this period that Pontiac began transforming its image from a solid, reliable car to that of a solid, reliable car with fearsome performance. It started in 1956 with the available 285-horsepower 316-cubic-inch V-8, and grew in '57 with the introduction of the Bonneville. All other models that year came with an enlarged 347-cid V-8 with 227 to 290 hp, but the flashy Bonneville got a 370-cid version with fuel injection and a rousing 310 hp. Available only as a convertible, the $5782 Bonneville cost nearly $2700 more than a Star Chief ragtop. Not surprisingly, just 630 were sold. **3.** Pontiacs got revised styling for '57 that gave them rear-slanted tailfins and a sleeker, more modern look, as evidenced by this $3481 Star Chief Safari two-door hardtop wagon. Sadly, it would prove to be the final year for this attractive body style. **4.** Chieftain was Pontiac's entry-level model, but in $2529 Catalina two-door coupe form, certainly didn't look it. **5.** Even Pontiac's conventional four-door wagons took the Safari name—and conventional Pontiac tail styling—for '57. Shown is the Star Chief version, which cost $155 more than its two-door hardtop sibling.

5

SCORECARD		1957
MAKE	TOTAL PRODUCTION	RANK
BUICK	404,049 ▼	4th ▼
CADILLAC	146,841 ▼	9th ●
CHEVROLET	1,505,910 ▼	2nd ▼
OLDSMOBILE	384,390 ▼	5th ●
PONTIAC	333,473 ▼	6th ●

1

2

1. Buick went baroque in 1958 with an ornate grille housing 160 shiny squares, along with pointed tailfins overlaying gaudy chrome side panels. To many, this was just too much, even for the flashy Fifties. Surely a blinding sight when the sun was shining, this Roadmaster convertible went for $4680. **2.** Uniquely trimmed—but no less conspicuous—was the top-line Limited hardtop coupe at $5002. **3.** Cadillacs weren't exactly wallflowers themselves for 1958, gaining taller, pointed tailfins and the quad headlamps worn by most every car that year. This Series 62 convertible cost $5454. **4.** For another $2000, a buyer could opt for the specialty Eldorado convertible with the same unique tailfins it wore for '57. Only 815 folks anted up the extra cash. **5.** A long-wheelbase $6232 Cadillac Sixty Special would take a back seat to nobody in a no-holds-barred contest of chrome.

3

4

5

1

2

3

4

5

1. A drastic redesign greeted Chevy buyers for 1958. Newly installed as the top-line model that year was the Impala, technically a subseries of the Bel Air line. It was offered only as a convertible or a hardtop coupe, shown here. In V-8 form, they were priced at $2841 and $2693, respectively. Six-cylinder versions cost about $100 less. Note the three taillights on each side that, during the 1960s, would come to signify an Impala; lesser models had one or two. **2.** One of those "lesser models" was the regular Bel Air. In two-door-sedan form, it cost $200 less than a comparable Impala. Joining the 235-cubic-inch six and 283-cid V-8 for '58 was a new 348-cid V-8. This "big-block" (as opposed to the "small-block" 283) was a converted truck engine, and offered from 250 to 315 horsepower. **3.** For 1958, Chevy's former entry-level 150 series was renamed Delray, a moniker previously used on a midline 210 coupe. Two-door Delray sedans such as this one started as low as $2013. Replacing the midline 210 was the Biscayne, which—model for model—cost about $135 more than a Delray. **4-5.** Corvette adopted quad-headlight styling for 1958, which also brought a revised grille. Unique to this model year were slotted hood vents and dual chrome trunklid spears, easy ways to tell a '58 from any other model. The popularity of Chevy's sports car was growing every year, and even a substantial price hike for '58 didn't slow that down. At $3631, a Corvette cost nearly $800 more than the most expensive Impala convertible.

1. A solid contender for the King of Bling in '58 was the redesigned Oldsmobile—especially in top-line Ninety-Eight trim. This chrome-encrusted convertible cost $4300. Underhood, the available J-2 engine option for the 371-cubic-inch V-8 now yielded 312 horsepower. **2.** Sharing the Ninety-Eight's glitzy trim was the Super 88, which rode a 3.3-inch-shorter wheelbase. It's represented here by the $3529 convertible. **3.** Not quite as blindingly bright was the base Olds, newly named Dynamic 88. This Holiday hardtop coupe cost $2893. **4.** The Super 88 Fiesta hardtop wagon was a fast and flashy hauler at $3623.

1

2

3

4

1

2

4

1-2. Pontiacs received a total makeover for 1958, and like its GM siblings, piled on the chrome. Nowhere was this more evident than in the top-line Bonneville, which now rode the shorter Chieftain wheelbase and added a two-door hardtop to the existing convertible. A monumental $2200 price cut put the convertible at $3586; the coupe cost $3481. **3.** Pontiac's new quad-headlight front end took center stage, but also new was that all models got the 370-cubic V-8 previously reserved for Bonnevilles. It produced from 240 to 300 horse-power, or 310 in Bonneville's fuel-injected version. A Bonneville convertible (shown) paced that year's Indy 500. **4.** Safari station wagons appeared in the low-line Chieftain and top-line Star Chief series. Only the Chieftain offered a third-row seat. This Star Chief Safari went for $3350, about $330 more than a comparable Chieftain.

3

SCORECARD		1958
MAKE	TOTAL PRODUCTION	RANK
BUICK	240,659 ▾	5th ▾
CADILLAC	121,778 ▾	10th ▾
CHEVROLET	1,142,460 ▾	1st ▴
OLDSMOBILE	314,374 ▾	4th ▴
PONTIAC	216,982 ▾	6th ●

1

2

3

1-2. In a stunning aesthetic reversal, Buick peeled chrome from its completely restyled '59s. Not so with tailfins, however, which increased in size and number. The rears became huge canted wings, a look that was mirrored in front. Model names were changed, too: LeSabre, Invicta, Electra, and Electra 225 made up the new order. The closed models depicted are four-door hardtops, which had a distinctive "flat-top" profile and huge wraparound rear window. **3.** Four-door pillared sedans had a completely different roofline that incorporated thin pillars and a conventional tapered look. This entry-level LeSabre sedan went for $2804. **4.** Nothing showed off Buick's new jet-age styling like a blazing red Electra 225 convertible. The $4192 rag-top seemed to be flying just standing still. **5.** An Electra 225 convertible that really *did* fly was the pace car for the 1959 running of the Indy 500. New for all Buicks but the entry-level LeSabre was a 325-horsepower 401-cubic-inch V-8; LeSabre kept the 250-hp 364. Buick's long-held "doctor's car" reputation sustained it through the end of the twentieth century and beyond, even if the cars bearing the Buick name weren't always the flamboyant carriages that closed out the '50s.

4

5

1

2

3

4

5

1. Towering tailfins with twin bullet taillights marked the 1959 Cadillacs—and made them famous. You could have a pair of your very own affixed to a Series 62 convertible for $5455. **2.** Eldorado eschewed its traditional unique tailfins for more-pronounced versions of those found on lesser Caddys, thanks to a thick chrome trim strip that started at the windshield pillar and flowed to the tail. Eldorado's $7401 price added nearly $2000 to the cost of a comparable Series 62. **3.** Not to be outdone, front ends took on an equally flamboyant look, with "eyebrowed" headlights and a chrome-studded grille. **4.** The exclusive Eldorado Brougham was restyled, with production turned over to Pinin Farina in Italy. None of this made it any cheaper: It still listed for an astronomical $13,075. **5.** Cadillac's rocketship styling is modeled by a $7401 Eldorado Seville hardtop coupe. Cadillac remains GM's luxury division to this day, and typically leads all other domestic luxury cars in sales.

1. Since Chevrolets had been completely restyled for 1958 and then completely restyled *again* for '59, they were indeed "All New All Over Again," as this ad states. Depicted is the flat-top four-door hardtop, a roof style shared with other GM cars that year. **2.** Chevy's "batwing" tailfins really stood out—in more ways than one. Impala was now a proper model perched at the top of the lineup, and this V-8 Impala convertible could have flown into your garage for $2967. **3.** The midline Bel Air drew the most sales, and though a four-door hardtop was offered, the $2440 pillared sedan cost $116 less. **4.** Aside from stripping off the hood slats and trunk spears, there were few changes to the $3875 Corvette. **5.** In a delayed reaction to the car-based Ford Ranchero that appeared two years earlier, 1959 saw the debut of the El Camino; a name—and concept—that would live on into the '80s. It was billed as "a vehicle combining ultra style with utility," and indeed it did. Chevrolet was the best-selling brand through most of the 1950s, and even in a changed market that has since seen an invasion of imports, it still holds that distinction today.

ALL NEW ALL OVER AGAIN!

'59 CHEVROLET

1

2

3

4

5

1

2

1. Like its GM siblings, Oldsmobiles were redesigned for 1959, gaining "Quiet power...extra safety...a Glide Ride...and Linear Look"—or so said the ads. **2.** The "flat-top" four-door hardtop sedan looked particularly good dressed in Oldsmobile's aforesaid "Linear Look." This top-line Ninety-Eight version went for $4162 with the division's new 315-horsepower 394-cubic-inch V-8 that was shared with the Super 88. **3.** The Ninety-Eight convertible topped Oldsmobile's price scale at $4366. **4.** A Ninety-Eight pillared sedan listed for $3890, $272 less than its hardtop sibling. Oldsmobile would continue its reputation as an engineering leader through the 1960s, and for a couple of years in the '70s, produced the nation's best-selling car. But Olds began to lose its luster in the '80s as GM "genericized" its brands for cost savings, and after celebrating its 100th anniversary in 1997, was unceremoniously dropped after the 2004 model year. It was a sad end for what was once a brilliant star.

3

4

1. A 1959 reskin brought the "Wide-Track Pontiac," a slogan the division would use well into the '60s. But it wasn't just advertising hype: Tread width increased by 4.5 inches in the rear and a whopping five inches in front. Adding visual width to a car that was already plenty wide enough was a low, split grille that tapered at the nose and extended fully across the front end. After a one-year hiatus for 1960, the split grille would return, becoming a Pontiac trademark that was used in one form or another on most of the division's cars through the 1980s, and graces every new Pontiac sold today. Shown is the top-line $3586 Bonneville convertible. **2-4.** The Bonneville series—which had previously consisted only of convertible and two-door hardtop "sporty" models—expanded to include a "flat-top" four-door hardtop sedan and even a station wagon for 1959. Low, wide taillight lenses mimicked the look in front, and were chosen for the same reason: to add the appearance of great girth. The flat-top sedan, two-door hardtop, and station wagon listed for $3333, $3257, and $3532, respectively. **5.** If a (rather costly) Bonneville wasn't in the cards, the $2704 price of entry to a Catalina four-door pillared sedan might be more palatable. A comparable midline Star Chief was about $300 more. All '59 Pontiacs were fitted with a larger 389-cubic-inch V-8 that put out 215 to 303 horsepower, or up to 345 hp with the triple two-barrel carburetor setup known as Tri-Power. Features such as a wide-track stance and powerful Tri-Power engines earned Pontiac a performance reputation that hit its stride during the Sixties, and continues to this day.

1

2

3

5

4

Hudson Motor Car Company was founded in 1909 by a group of businessmen that included Roy D. Chapin, Sr., and retailing magnate Joseph L. Hudson. The former became the company's first president; the latter lent his name to the product.

The Hudson badge adorned some of America's fleetest and finest cars during the company's history, but a lower-price companion make—first called Essex, then Terraplane after 1933—helped Hudson survive the Depression. These models were folded into the Hudson line in the late Thirties, and the Terraplane name was dropped.

Though Hudson wasn't the first company to use what we now call unitized construction, it introduced a new twist with its redesigned 1948 models. Marketed as the "Step-down" design, it surrounded the passenger compartment with integrated frame girders, thus allowing the floor to be lower than in other cars of the day. This resulted in a high degree of passenger protection and a lower center of gravity. The latter was at least as responsible as the company's famed Twin H-Power six-cylinder engine in helping the Hudson Hornet rule the stock-car tracks in its heyday. Unfortunately, it also made the car expensive to update, a problem that would plague Hudson after the postwar seller's boom subsided in the early '50s. As sales dwindled, Hudson was forced to merge with Nash in 1954 to form American Motors Corporation (see separate entry), but neither marque would live to see the end of the decade.

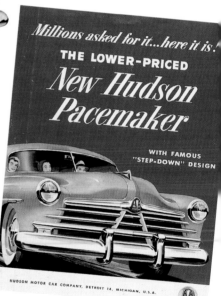

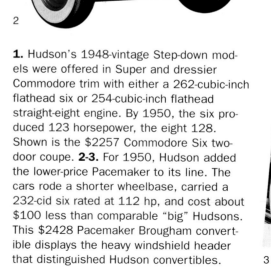

1. Hudson's 1948-vintage Step-down models were offered in Super and dressier Commodore trim with either a 262-cubic-inch flathead six or 254-cubic-inch flathead straight-eight engine. By 1950, the six produced 123 horsepower, the eight 128. Shown is the $2257 Commodore Six two-door coupe. **2-3.** For 1950, Hudson added the lower-price Pacemaker to its line. The cars rode a shorter wheelbase, carried a 232-cid six rated at 112 hp, and cost about $100 less than comparable "big" Hudsons. This $2428 Pacemaker Brougham convertible displays the heavy windshield header that distinguished Hudson convertibles. 3

1-2. Hudson greeted 1951 with a new arched grille, and offered General Motors' Hydra-Matic automatic transmission as an option. But the big news was the introduction of what would become a stock-car legend: the Hornet. Based on the longer Super/Commodore chassis, the Hornet's distinguishing feature was a huge 308-cubic-inch version of the flathead six, making it the biggest six of the era. It put out 145 horsepower, 17 more than the company's smaller straight eight, and ten more than Oldsmobile's renowned overhead-valve V-8. This newfound power, combined with the Step-down's lower center of gravity and superior handling, resulted in the first of what would become a long string of stock-car racing victories. This Hornet four-door sedan listed for $2568. 3. Also new for '51 was a two-door hardtop body style, which gave the big Hudsons a much airier look. It was offered in all series except the low-price Pacemaker; shown is the $2869 Hornet version.

1

2

3

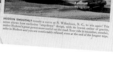

1-2. Hudson took "only" 13 stock-car victories during 1951, but racked up a stunning 49 wins in 1952. No doubt the introduction of the company's Twin H-Power dual carburetor setup had something to do with that. Most often fitted to the Hornet's 308-cubic-inch six, it gave Hudson yet another advantage on the track. **3.** Though the two-door hardtop was flashier, the lighter, cheaper two-door club coupe was the hot Hornet to have—and what most racers drove on the track. However, "cheaper" was relative; this '52 Hornet club coupe listed for $2742 ($353 less than the hardtop), which made it about $400 more than an Oldsmobile Super 88, and nearly $300 more than a Buick Super hardtop. Replacing Hudson's own "Super"— the Super Six—was the Wasp. Built on the shorter Pacemaker wheelbase but powered by the larger 262-cid six from the Commodore Six, it offered performance second only to the Hornet in Hudson's line at nearly $300 less. In a 1952 styling change, taillights went from vertical to horizontal.

1

1. Hudson simplified its model lineup for 1953. What had been the Pacemaker took on the Wasp name, the former Wasp became the Super Wasp, and the Hornet became the lone long-wheelbase flagship, as the equally priced Commodore Eight was dropped. Shown is a Super Wasp in two-door sedan form, a body style not offered in Hornet trim. 2-3. In an effort to duplicate Nash's success with the compact Rambler, Hudson brought out the compact Jet for 1953. Unfortunately, sales never took off. Part of the problem was the car's tall, ungainly look, and part was the price: The cheapest Jet cost $1858—nearly $200 more than a base full-size Chevrolet—and this better-trimmed Super Jet four-door sedan listed for $1954. All Jets were powered by a 202-cubic-inch six. Developing the Jet cost a bundle that Hudson couldn't afford to lose, and the car's failure likely forced the company's merger with Nash.

3

2

SCORECARD		1950-53
YEAR	TOTAL PRODUCTION	RANK
1950	121,408 ▼	13th ▼
1951	131,915 ▲	13th ●
1952	70,000 ▼	14th ▼
1953	66,143 ▼	15th ▼

Conceived during the postwar years when a shortage of new cars made it a seller's market, Kaiser-Frazer Corporation joined the fray as perhaps the most viable automaker among the growing number of independents. Founded by shipbuilder Henry J. Kaiser and super salesman Joseph W. Frazer, each lent their name to separate cars that were nearly identical save for trim variations and price. Kaisers and Frazers were rather large and expensive—roughly the size and cost of a top-line V-8 Oldsmobile 98—yet were powered by a lowly flat-head six-cylinder engine. If it weren't for the huge pent-up demand, it's doubtful the company would have even gotten off the ground. As it was, however, the pair sold a combined 140,000 cars in inaugural 1947, a strong showing.

But by 1950, the tide was already turning. Both makes were fading, particularly the more expensive Frazer, which would bow out after a brief run of 1951 models. That same year, Kaiser branched out with a companion make, the compact Henry J. It, too, sold strongly at first, then nosedived to a 1954 death. Kaiser attempted to replace it with another compact, the acquired Aero-Willys, but both makes finally called it quits during 1955. It was a grand experiment, and to the company's credit, it outlasted any of the other postwar independents.

1

2

3

4

1. Both Kaiser and Frazer sold leftover 1949 models as 1950s. Each line offered two trim levels, with Frazers being slightly pricier than comparable Kaisers. The '50 Frazer four-door sedan cost $2395 in standard form (shown), $200 more in uplevel Manhattan guise. All Kaiser-Frazer models were powered by a 226-cubic-inch flathead six designed by Continental but built by K-F; it produced 100 horsepower in low-line models, 112 in upper-line series. **2.** Kaiser beat most automakers to market with a four-door hardtop. Called the Virginian, it wasn't a *true* hardtop, as the center roof pillar was replaced by a framed glass pane that didn't roll down like the other windows. At $2995, it cost $800 more than a comparable sedan, and few were sold. **3.** Another innovative body style was the utility sedan, with an upper hatch lid and lower tailgate replacing the traditional trunklid. Folding the rear seatback created a long load area complete with wood floor ribbing. This Kaiser Vagabond retailed for $2288, just $93 more than a conventional sedan. **4.** K-F was known for offering a wide variety of vivid exterior hues, and interiors of higher-line models in particular could be adorned with extensive chrome trim and rich, colorful fabrics.

1

2

1. A 1951 restyle with dipped beltline, squared-off rear fenders, and oddly shaped rear roof pillars gave Kaisers a fresh look. Also new that year was a Dragon trim option—shown here—that included special exterior colors, a padded vinyl top, and alligator-look vinyl interior. **2.** Frazers were also restyled for 1951, but this time, there was more distinction between the two makes. Frazer belatedly got a four-door hardtop, the $3075 Manhattan. It joined a convertible version—by then the only four-door ragtop on the market besides the similar Kaiser version—that had sold in very small numbers since 1949. Also newly available was GM's Hydra-Matic automatic transmission. However, none of this was enough to keep Frazer alive, and the name faded away after '51. **3.** Henry J. Kaiser felt a compact would give him a car the Big Three didn't offer, and since he'd already used the name "Kaiser," he called this one...the "Henry J." It arrived for 1951 in four- and six-cylinder versions priced from $1363 to $1499. First-year sales topped 80,000 units, but it would be all downhill from there. **4.** Kaisers displayed a revised grille and model line for '52, but little else was new. This top-line Manhattan (a name borrowed from defunct Frazer) went for $2654.

3

4

1

2

3

4

5

1-2. A 1953 Henry J shows off the facelift it got for '52. Also added at that time was a trunklid, which was previously absent. Prices now ranged from $1399 to $1561. Some unsold 1953 models were reserialed and sold as '54s, after which the Henry J was put out to pasture. **3.** Dragon trim was revived for a 1953 Kaiser of the same name, which listed for a pricey $3924. It wore gold-plated ornamentation along with a padded top and distinct interior materials. **4.** More reasonable was the '53 Kaiser Deluxe Traveller at $2619. **5.** Despite its financial problems, the company produced a handful of fiberglass-bodied Kaiser-Darrin sports cars for 1954. Using leftover chassis and 90-horsepower six-cylinder engines from the departed Henry J, it had a novel sliding side door and a steep $3668 price, which attracted only 435 buyers. **6.** Kaisers received a facelift for 1954, and top-line Manhattans got a 140-hp supercharged version of the 226-cubic-inch six. This four-door version carried a $2670 price tag.

6

1

2

3

4

1. Still believing in the viability of compact cars, Henry J. Kaiser bought Willys-Overland in 1954, which got him the little Willys Aero. The Aero was larger than the Henry J but also more expensive; the cheapest four-cylinder Aero Lark (shown) cost $1737, which could easily buy a larger six-cylinder Chevrolet. Aero also offered a six-cylinder engine—two actually: a 191-cubic-inch Willys with 90 horsepower, and Kaiser's own 226-cid with 115 hp. **2.** A lone Manhattan carried the Kaiser banner into 1955, but a mild "taillift" wasn't enough to save it, and Kaiser bowed out. **3-4.** Willys got a revised grille for 1955, when four-cylinder versions were dropped. Added as a top-line model was the Bermuda, shown here in two-door hardtop form. These sporty-looking models sold for $1895 to $1997, far too much to be popular. The Willys Aero died in the United States along with Kaiser, but other Willys products under the Jeep name would transfer to other owners, and of course, the name continues to this day.

SCORECARD		1950-55
YEAR/MAKE	TOTAL PRODUCTION	RANK
1950		
KAISER	15,228 ▼	17th ▼
FRAZER	3,700 ▼	19th ▼
1951		
KAISER	139,452 ▲	12th ▲
FRAZER	10,214 ▲	19th ●
HENRY J	81,942	17th
1952		
KAISER	32,131 ▼	16th ▼
HENRY J	30,585 ▼	18th ▼
WILLYS	31,363	17th
1953		
KAISER	27,652 ▼	18th ▼
HENRY J	16,672 ▼	19th ▼
WILLYS	42,057 ▲	16th ▲
1954		
KAISER	8,539 ▼	18th ●
WILLYS	11,856 ▼	17th ▼
1955		
KAISER	1,291 ▼	19th ▼
WILLYS	6,565 ▼	18th ▼

After cutting his automotive teeth at General Motors, Charles W. Nash left the corporation in 1916 to form his own company and bring out a car under his own name. Nash built mainly midpriced cars that often sported innovative features. Among them was the 1941 600, one of the earlier cars with unitized construction. These and other Nashes of the '40s carried somewhat unusual styling, but that changed in 1949 with the introduction of the "bathtub" Airflytes, which went from "unusual" to just plain weird.

Smooth where other cars of the day were lumpy, Airflytes looked aerodynamic and they were. Aiding this in both appearance and fact were skirted fenders that made Nashes unmistakable, a signature trait they would maintain until the bitter end.

But as the company entered the Fifties, the bitter end was nowhere in sight. Airflytes were selling well, and they inspired the styling of Nash's new compact, the Rambler. One of the few small cars that actually proved popular during that period, the Rambler would be shared with partner Hudson after the 1954 merger that formed American Motors Corporation (see entry), and eventually go on to outlive Nash itself.

1

2

3

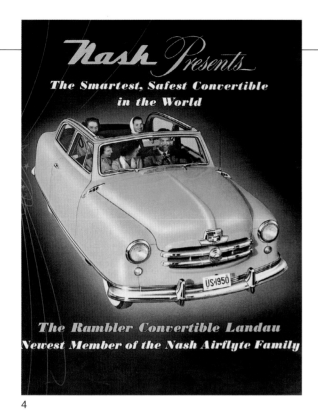

4

5

6

1-3. It isn't hard to guess where the "bathtub" Airflytes got their nickname. Topping the 1950 Nash lineup were the long-wheelbase Ambassadors (shown), which came as two- and four-door sedans in a host of trim levels with prices ranging from $2039 to $2223. GM's Hydra-Matic automatic transmission was newly optional. Sharing the look, but on a shorter wheelbase, was the $1633 to $1897 Statesman. Ambassadors had a 234-cubic-inch six with 112 horsepower, Statesmans a 184-cid version with 82 hp. Both models were known for having seats that folded down into a bed. **4-6.** New for 1950 was the compact Rambler, which carried many "big Nash" styling cues. It was initially offered in two unusual body styles—a two-door all-steel wagon and a Landau convertible with fold-back top and stationary side windows—both priced at $1808 and powered by a 172-cid six with 82 hp.

1

2

3

1. Though they aided aerodynamics and contributed to the car's unique look, the Rambler's skirted fenders made for a large turning circle and cumbersome flat-tire changes—problems that also afflicted the larger Nashes, and for the same reason. At $1993, the 1951 Rambler convertible sold surprisingly well considering a full-size Chevrolet convertible cost only $37 more. **2.** There was a greater price spread between a 1951 Rambler wagon and those sold by the Big Three—mostly because the Big Three's were all "woodys." This Rambler Custom went for $1993, but the cheaper Super was just $1885. By contrast, Big Three wagons ranged from $2029 to $2191. **3.** New to the Rambler lineup for '51 was the $1968 Custom Country Club hardtop coupe. It introduced the reverse-slant rear roof pillar that would later appear in Nash's larger cars.

1-2. A 1951 facelift brought big Nashes a vertical-bar grille (in place of crosshatch) and peaked rear fenders. **3.** A definite family resemblance can be seen in this 1951 Nash brochure showing (left to right) a Rambler, Statesman, and Ambassador. **4.** A collaborative effort between Nash and Donald Healey of England resulted in the aptly named Nash-Healey sports car. With an aluminum body and 125-horsepower version of the Ambassador engine, it was a vivid performer, but just 104 were sold at a steep $4063.

1

2

Nash Presents the World's Most Modern Cars, the 1951 Airflytes

3

4

1

2

3

4

5

6

1-2. In celebration of Nash's 50th anniversary, the redesigned 1952 full-size models were promoted as "Golden Airflytes," though they appeared to take a step backward in the aerodynamics department. Styled in part by the famed Italian design house of Pinin Farina, they kept Nash's trademark unibody construction and skirted fenders, but adopted a squarer profile and a conventional roofline with reverse-slant rear window. Added to the line was a two-door hardtop. Ambassadors got a power boost via a larger 252-cubic-inch six with 120 horsepower. **3-4.** This Statesman Custom four-door sedan cost $2332 with its 88-hp six. **5-6.** Unlike their big brothers, the little Ramblers didn't change much for 1952. **7.** Though the small sales volume could hardly justify it, the Nash-Healey was restyled for '52. Another Pinin Farina effort, it had a steel body with a one-piece windshield, headlights moved inboard and encircled by an oval grille, and a kick-up added to the rear fenders. A Nash-Healey won its class at LeMans.

7

1. Ramblers got a squared-up front end for 1953 that made them more closely resemble their bigger brothers. Two new six-cylinder engines were offered: an 85-horsepower 184-cubic-inch version with manual transmission, and a 90-hp 195-cid with automatic. This convertible topped the range at $2150. **2.** Statesman's engine was bumped to 100 hp for '53, when this two-door Super sold for $2143. **3.** Nash ads promoted the '53 Statesman and Ambassador as "Pinin Farina's latest styling triumph," but in fact, they were little-changed in appearance from 1952. What *was* new was optional power steering and a dual-carbureted version of the Ambassador's 252-cubic-inch six, which added 20 horsepower for a total of 140. **4.** A LeMans coupe version of the Nash-Healey was added for 1953. It rode a longer wheelbase than the convertible and was priced even higher: $6399 vs. $5908. Nash's story would continue under American Motors Corporation (see separate entry), which was formed when the company merged with Hudson in early 1954.

1

2

3

4

SCORECARD		1950-53
YEAR	TOTAL PRODUCTION	RANK
1950	171,782 ▲	11th ▼
1951	205,307 ▲	10th ▲
1952	154,291 ▼	10th ●
1953	121,793 ▼	12th ▼

Sometimes it's hard to understand how a company that once so clearly dominated its market segment could sink so far so fast. Yet such was the case with Packard.

Started in 1899 by James Ward Packard, the company quickly grew to become a prominent automaker. By 1930 it was by far the most popular luxury make, with more than double the sales of Cadillac. And in 1940, it outsold "The Standard of the World" by a seven-to-one margin. It wasn't until after World War II that Cadillac finally caught it, and then the two companies played "who's in first" for a couple of years before Packard took a nosedive into oblivion.

Some blame the make's fall on its slow transition away from medium-priced models that were introduced to weather the Depression. By 1950, Packard's most popular series was the Eight, which sold in the $2200 to $2400 price range—well below the cheapest Cadillacs. This put them up against such midpriced powerhouses as Buick, Chrysler, and Mercury, a formidable segment. Super Eight and Custom Eight were the senior models, but by this time, their sales were but a trickle. Packard rallied briefly, then merged with a sinking Studebaker in 1954 to form Studebaker-Packard Corporation (see separate entry), which ended up dragging the grand marque to the bottom.

5

1. Packard's top-line model for 1950 was the Custom Eight, offered only in four-door sedan and convertible forms. Production was very limited: just 707 of the $3875 sedans, and only 77 of the $4570 convertibles. 2. Introduced in late 1949 was Ultramatic Drive, Packard's first automatic transmission. 3-4. Packard's volume car was called simply the "Eight." Riding a shorter wheelbase than other models, it was offered in two- and four-door sedans priced from $2224 to $2383, along with a $3449 "woody" wagon. 5-6. A 1950 Packard brochure shows the complete lineup. Entry-level Eights wore a horizontal-bar grille, top-line Customs a crosshatch grille. In between sat the mid-line Supers, which rode the longer wheelbase and had mixed grille patterns: Base Supers had the Eight's grille, Deluxe models the Custom's grille. Due to their bulbous styling, Packards of this era were often derided as "pregnant elephants." Note Packard's famous cormorant hood ornament, which is depicted only slightly out of scale in these illustrations. All Packards were powered by a flathead straight-eight engine, but in different displacements and power ratings for each series. The Eight's 288-cubic-inch version made 135 horsepower, the Super's 327 had 150 hp, and the Custom's 356 made 160 hp—the most offered in an American car for 1950.

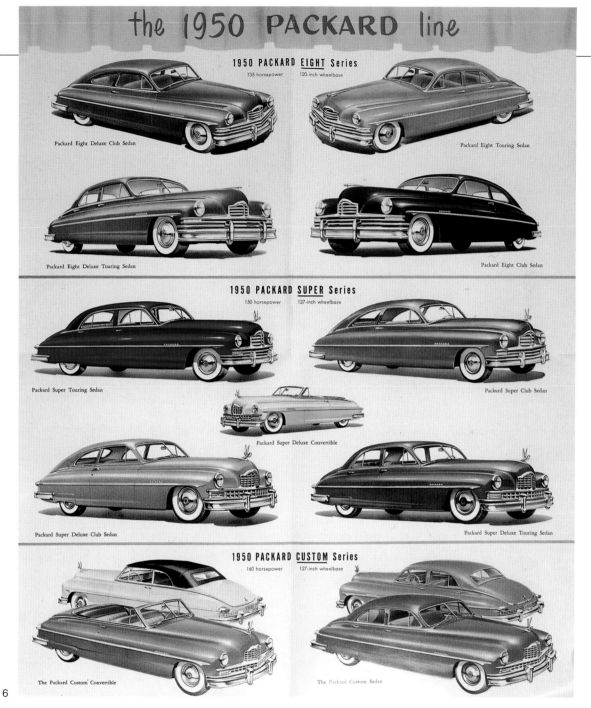

the 1950 PACKARD line

1950 PACKARD EIGHT Series
135 horsepower   120-inch wheelbase

Packard Eight Deluxe Club Sedan

Packard Eight Touring Sedan

Packard Eight Deluxe Touring Sedan

Packard Eight Club Sedan

1950 PACKARD SUPER Series
150 horsepower   127-inch wheelbase

Packard Super Touring Sedan

Packard Super Club Sedan

Packard Super Deluxe Convertible

Packard Super Deluxe Club Sedan

Packard Super Deluxe Touring Sedan

1950 PACKARD CUSTOM Series
160 horsepower   127-inch wheelbase

The Packard Custom Convertible

The Packard Custom Sedan

6

1

2

3

1. Packards boasted an all-new look for 1951 that earned them "the most beautiful car of the year" award from the Society of Motion Picture Art Directors. The redesign more than doubled sales, but the company still slightly trailed Cadillac. Packards also got new model names. The base series was now the 200, followed by the 250, 300, and top-line Patrician 400. The 200 and 250 sat on a shorter wheelbase than the 300 and 400. Engines carried over, though the big 356-cubic-inch eight was dropped. The 200 had the 288 cid with 135 hp, all others the 327 with 150-155 hp. **2.** A new body style was the Mayfair hardtop coupe, available only in the 250 series for $3234. **3.** The top-line Patrician 400 could be identified by its added chrome trim and different taillight treatment. It came only as this $3662 four-door sedan.

1

3

2

1. Aside from newly available power steering, Packards carried into 1952 with few changes. Now that all its rivals had modern overhead-valve V-8s, Packard's famously smooth but increasingly antiquated flathead straight eight was beginning to be a detriment to sales—which indeed dropped significantly for '52. **2-3.** The 250 series consisted of just two body styles, both available only in this series. The 250 Mayfair hardtop coupe and 250 convertible were priced at $3318 and $3476, respectively, and together accounted for a mere 5200 sales. By far the biggest seller was Packard's entry-level 200 series, but the popularity of these midpriced cars only served to further dilute the company's luxury image.

1

3

2

1-2. Packard tried to differentiate its high-priced cars from the midpriced lines for 1953 by renaming the latter Clipper and Clipper Deluxe; the bigger cars were now Cavalier and Patrician. **3.** New for '53 was the elaborately decorated—and astronomically priced—Caribbean convertible. Among its identifying touches were radiused wheelwells heavily outlined in chrome, wire wheels, and a lack of side trim. Competing directly against similar specialty convertibles from General Motors, the Caribbean sold just 750 copies, but that was enough to beat Cadillac's Eldorado. Newly available on upper-line Packards was the Caribbean's new 180-horsepower version of the 327 straight eight.

1. Twice as many people bought a conventional $3486 Packard convertible as purchased the high-price Caribbean, thereby saving themselves $1724. 2. The $3244 Cavalier sedan rode the Patrician's "long" wheelbase, but cost $500 less. 3. Newly available on the $3278 Mayfair hardtop was an "outside spare" continental kit. 4. Packard's cheapest car for 1953 was the $2544 Clipper club sedan. Priced in Buick/Chrysler/Oldsmobile territory, Clippers accounted for the bulk of Packard sales. 5. At the other end of the spectrum was the $3740 Patrician sedan, which cost about the same as a Cadillac but sold in far lower volume. Packard sales were reasonably healthy—as was the company's financial status—when it merged with (actually bought) Studebaker in 1954, thereby forming the Studebaker-Packard Corporation. The story of both marques continues in that section.

SCORECARD		1950-53
YEAR	TOTAL PRODUCTION	RANK
1950	42,627 ▼	15th ▼
1951	100,713 ▲	16th ▼
1952	62,921 ▼	15th ▲
1953	90,252 ▲	14th ▲

Established in 1852 as a wagon maker, Studebaker began building cars in 1902. Early models spanned a broad price range, but by the 1940s, six-cylinder Studebakers were selling for Chevrolet prices, while eights were closer to Buick territory.

For the most part, Studebakers of the era displayed rather conventional styling—until 1950, when the famed "bullet-nose" appeared. Though controversial, the new look proved wildly popular, catapulting Studebaker from eleventh to eighth in industry sales virtually overnight. By this time, eight-cylinder versions had departed, leaving just a pair of economical sixes—though not for long.

But just as quickly as they had risen, Studebaker's fortunes soon began to sink. Saved from the brink by a Packard buyout in 1954, the new Studebaker-Packard Corporation (see entry) would see one of the partners fail, while the other would live on—at least for a time.

1

2

3

4

1. Styled to resemble the nose of an airplane, Studebaker's radical 1950 front end may look odd in today's light, but was a raging success at its introduction—and helped the company reach a record 320,000 sales. Also helping was Studebaker's first automatic transmission, optional on all models. The entry-level, 113-inch-wheelbase Champion line was powered by a 169-cubic-inch six rated at 85 horsepower; it's represented here by a $1981 Regal Deluxe convertible. **2.** Midpriced Commanders had a 120-inch wheelbase and a 245-cid six with 102 hp. That same engine powered the range-topping 124-inch-wheelbase Land Cruiser, shown here in $2187 four-door sedan form. **3.** The Champion's fuel economy is stressed in this ad. Its engine was much smaller than those in Chevrolets and Plymouths, and the Champion weighed less, too. **4.** Studebaker prices started at $1419 for this Champion Custom three-passenger coupe, putting it on par with the cheapest Chevys, Fords, and Plymouths.

1

New 120-horsepower V-8
Studebaker Commander

New peaks of power! New driving thrills!
A real gas saver! Needs no premium fuel!

2

3

1-2. The '51 Studebaker Commander's restyled grille looked as though it was smiling, and for good reason: Behind it lay a new overhead-valve V-8. Sized at 232 cubic inches, it put out 120 horsepower, making the Commander a weakling no more. The long-wheelbase Land Cruiser sedan enjoyed the same changes. Champions got the grille but not the V-8, as they retained their old 169-cid flathead six. Note this car's "suicide" rear doors, which had been adopted by all Studebaker four-door sedans in the 1950 redesign. **3.** An interesting body style offered by Studebaker was the Starlight coupe, with its wraparound, four-piece rear window. Some questioned whether the cars were "coming or going," but there was little question that they were unique. The coupe was offered in the Champion (shown) and Commander lines in a total of five trim levels, with prices ranging from $1561 to $2137.

2

1

1-2. Small hoods tacked over the top of the taillights identified '52 Studebakers from the rear, but the real change was up front. Gone was the popular but controversial bullet-nose, replaced by a low, wide, "toothy" grille that prompted the nickname "clam digger." **3.** A Commander convertible paced the 1952 running of the Indianapolis 500, the only time during the decade an independent automaker was given that honor. It was a fitting way to celebrate Studebaker's 100th anniversary. **4.** An ad stresses the "Jet-streamed styling and standout gas saving" of the 1952 models. A Commander convertible was given center stage, but in the lower right corner was pictured a '52 newcomer: the Starliner hardtop coupe, which was offered in the Champion and Commander lines. The former cost $2220, the latter $2488, both about $280 more than the conventional coupes.

3

4

1-3. A stately 1952 Commander sedan shows off its chrome-trimmed instrument panel and "suicide" rear doors—so named because with the car parked at the curb, passengers exiting the street-side rear seat risked being crushed by the door if it was struck by a vehicle coming from behind. Whitewall tires and the wing-shaped front bumper guard were options. Commander sedans were offered in Regal or State trim, priced at $2121 and $2208, respectively. **4.** Calling the restyled 1952 models the "newest of the new," this ad fails to mention that they wouldn't be "new" for long. The clam-digger design lasted but a year, making a '52 Studebaker easy to spot—which wasn't such a great thing in '53.

1

2

3

4

1. Studebakers were redesigned for 1953, with straight-through rear fenders and a sloped nose. Four-door models abandoned their suicide rear doors for conventional ones, as shown on this Land Cruiser, which remained the top-line sedan and again rode a longer wheelbase—now 120.5 inches. **2.** Six-cylinder Champion and V-8 Commander sedans now sat on the same 116.5-inch wheelbase. **3-4.** Sharing the Land Cruiser's stretched chassis were rakish new Starlight pillared coupes. Whether in six-cylinder Champion or V-8 Commander guise, their long, low silhouette and smooth lines put them light-years ahead of other American cars in terms of styling, and earned them a Fashion Academy Award.

Exciting new 1953 *Studebaker*
receives *Fashion Academy Award!*

Gold medal for outstanding design and distinctive styling presented to the new American car with the European look

1

2

3

4

1

2

3

4

1-5. Even sleeker than the Starlight pillared coupe was the Starliner hardtop coupe. Starliners cost $161 more than Starlights and were likewise offered in both the Champion and Commander lines. As a Champion with the 85-horsepower 169-cubic-inch six, it went for $2116, while in Commander form with the 120-hp 232-cid V-8, it listed for $2374—making it Studebaker's most expensive model. Shown is the Commander Starliner, with V-8 badges on its hood, rear flanks, and trunklid. The rear view shows the oblong vertical taillights fitted to all '53 Studebakers. Whether in pillared or hardtop form, these beautiful cars are often referred to as the "Loewy coupes," after Studebaker's head of styling, Raymond Loewy. But they were actually the work of Bob Bourke, who had also penned Studebaker's 1950 bullet-nose models. But as coveted as these cars are today, they didn't help Studebaker's plight much in 1953. Sales had been steadily dropping since 1950's high of 320,000, and by this time, they were less than half that. And due to productivity problems at Studebaker's high-overhead South Bend, Indiana, plant, the company needed to build 250,000 cars a year just to break even. Three steady years of red ink with no color change in sight forced Studebaker to seek a saviour, and found it in Packard Corporation. The two merged in 1954 to form the Studebaker-Packard Corporation (see separate entry), where the story of both marques continued.

5

SCORECARD		1950-53
YEAR	TOTAL PRODUCTION	RANK
1950	320,884 ▲	8th ▲
1951	246,195 ▼	9th ▼
1952	167,662 ▼	9th ●
1953	151,576 ▼	10th ▼

Thanks to the success of its redesigned 1951 models, Packard was on fairly sound financial footing when it purchased moribund Studebaker in 1954. Unfortunately, Studebaker's many woes were not fully understood at the time of the buyout, and the flailing company pushed Packard ahead of it down the slippery slope to ruin.

But that, obviously, was not the initial plan. The Studebaker-Packard buyout was supposed to be a prelude to a Studebaker-Packard-Hudson-Nash merger intended to create a ladder-type corporation to rival Chrysler Corp., Ford Motor Co., and General Motors—thereby turning the Big Three into the Big Four. A relatively healthy Nash did its part by bailing out ailing Hudson, but the foursome never managed to pull off the bid. In both cases, sharing platforms was supposed to result in cost savings, when instead it just watered down each marque's appeal. Predictably, the "Packardbakers" that appeared for 1957 were far more attractive to Studebaker's customers than they were to Packard's, and it was the mother ship that first set sail to oblivion.

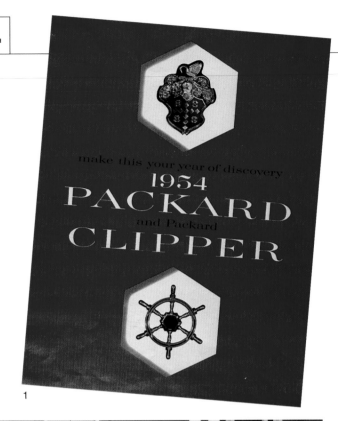

1

1-2. Packard had introduced the Clipper name in 1953 to denote its midpriced offerings, and they were by far the best-selling models. Topping the 1954 range was the $3125 Clipper Super Panama hardtop coupe, but other Clippers started as low as $2544. Clippers were identified by a unique tail treatment and slightly different grille. Depending on model, they packed either a 288-cubic-inch flathead straight eight with 150 horsepower, or a 327-cid with 165 hp. **3-4.** Packard's big cars rode a 127-inch wheelbase (vs. Clipper's 122), but three models carried "big car" styling on the shorter wheelbase: the standard convertible; a high-price, low-volume "deluxe" version of the convertible called the Caribbean; and the Pacific hardtop coupe. All three were powered by a new 359-cid straight eight with 212 hp, as was the top-line $3890 Patrician sedan. Also depicted in this brochure is the $3344 Cavalier, the Patrician's less expensive sibling, which carried a 327-cid straight eight with 185 hp. **5-6.** The Caribbean had been introduced in 1953 as a $5210 specialty convertible to rival similar cars from General Motors, and it continued for '54 with a staggering $6100 price tag. Only 400 were sold. **7.** A Pacific hardtop coupe went for $3827.

2

3

4

5

6

7

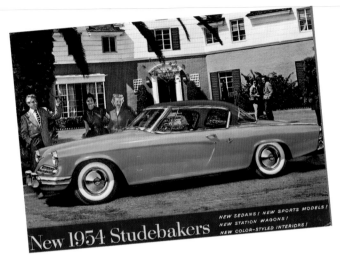

New 1954 Studebakers

NEW SEDANS! NEW SPORTS MODELS!
NEW STATION WAGONS!
NEW COLOR-STYLED INTERIORS!

1

2

3

1. Depicted on this 1954 brochure is Studebaker's beautiful Starliner hardtop coupe. Offered in both the Champion and top-line Commander series, they were priced at $2241 and $2502, respectively. All Champions were powered by a frugal 169-cubic-inch 85-horsepower flathead six, while Commanders got a 232-cid 127-hp overhead-valve V-8. **2.** Arriving for 1954 was Studebaker's first station wagon, the two-door Conestoga. It was available in both the Champion and Commander lines with prices ranging from $2187 to $2556. Both lines also offered two- and four-door sedans priced from $1758 to $2438. **3.** For $161 less than corresponding Starliner hardtop coupes, buyers could get a pillared Starlight coupe in either Champion or Commander trim.

SCORECARD		1954
MAKE	TOTAL PRODUCTION	RANK
PACKARD	31,291 ▼	16th ▼
STUDEBAKER	68,708 ▼	13th ▼

1. A deft facelift of the 1951-54 bodyshell resulted in what looked like an all-new Packard for 1955. Clippers kept their tail treatment but adopted a slightly altered version of the senior Packard's restyled front end. Also new were Torsion-Level ride, and—at last—a modern overhead-valve V-8. Two sizes went into Clippers: 320 cubic inches with 225 horsepower, or 352 cid with 245 hp. **2.** Topping the Clipper line was the $3076 Constellation hardtop coupe. Other Clippers could be had for as little as $2586.

1

2

1

2

3

4

1. With Packard's 1955 styling changes and new V-8 engine came renewed interest in its senior cars, which now included the Patrician sedan (shown in ad), Four Hundred hardtop coupe, and Caribbean convertible, all on a 127-inch wheelbase. This ad promotes Packard's new Torsion-Level suspension, which consisted of longitudinal torsion bars that replaced conventional coil springs and included a system for automatic leveling regardless of load. **2-3.** Packard's specialty convertible, the pricey Caribbean, was actually a little less pricey for 1955. It was rolled back from $6100 to $5932, despite having moved to the longer wheelbase. **4.** Completing the senior Packard line was the $3930 Four Hundred hardtop coupe. **5-6.** In a year when most every car sported a radical new look, Studebaker entered 1955 with warmed-over models...and sales inexplicably skyrocketed. The former long-wheelbase Land Cruiser sedan gave way to a line of two- and four-door models under the President name. Tops among them was the $3253 Speedster hardtop coupe, which was fitted with a new 259-cubic-inch V-8 making 185 horsepower; in other Presidents, it made 175 hp. Speedsters came with flamboyant two-tone paint, quilted leather upholstery, and an "engine-turned" instrument panel.

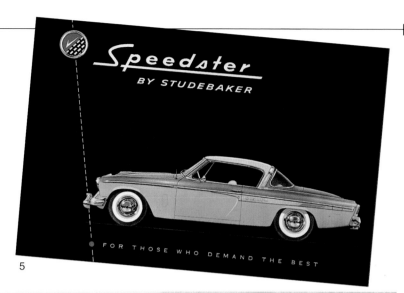

5

6

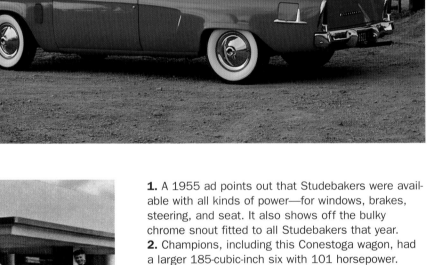

1. A 1955 ad points out that Studebakers were available with all kinds of power—for windows, brakes, steering, and seat. It also shows off the bulky chrome snout fitted to all Studebakers that year. **2.** Champions, including this Conestoga wagon, had a larger 185-cubic-inch six with 101 horsepower. Commanders started 1955 with a smaller 224-cid V-8 with 140 hp, but later in the model year got the President's 259 detuned to 162 hp. **3.** Champion four-door sedans were priced from $1783 to $1993—right in line with comparable Chevrolets.

SCORECARD		1955
MAKE	TOTAL PRODUCTION	RANK
PACKARD	55,247 ▲	14th ▲
STUDEBAKER	116,333 ▲	12th ▲

1

2

3

1-3. Clipper was made a separate make for 1956 and, having lost its Packard lineage, sales plummeted; ironic, because Clippers were now closer to the big Packards than ever before, as they no longer wore different taillights. Clipper was replaced in the lineup by the Executive, which shared the Clipper's body but had a "big Packard" grille and a bit more power: Both had a 352-cubic-inch V-8, but the Executive's made 275 horsepower vs. 240 hp for the Clipper. Executive was offered only as a four-door sedan or hardtop coupe (both shown). At $3465 for the sedan and $3560 for the coupe, prices sat about $400 to $600 north of comparable Clippers, $600 to $700 south of the big Patrician sedan and Four Hundred hardtop. It should have been popular, but wasn't: The Executive accounted for fewer than 3000 sales.

1

2

3

4

5

1. Packard's big cars made a mild comeback for 1956, but it was too little too late. Tops among Packard's closed models was the $4190 Four Hundred hardtop coupe; the Patrician sedan cost $30 less. Both were powered by a new 374-cubic-inch V-8—the biggest in the industry—making 290 horsepower. **2-3.** Still hanging on was the flamboyant Caribbean convertible, now joined by a hardtop version. Priced at $5995 and $5495, respectively, only about 270 of each were sold. Both carried a 310-hp version of the 374-cid V-8. These stately cars were the last of the "true" Packards, a sad but fitting farewell to a prestigious marque that had once been America's luxury leader. **4-5.** Mainline Studebakers were redesigned for 1956. Still on the same wheelbases, ads claimed they were bigger—and they looked it. Top-line Presidents got a new 289-cid V-8 with 195-225 horsepower; Commanders kept a 259 with 170-185 hp, Champions a 185-cid six with 101. Wagons were available in each series under the names Pinehurst, Parkview, and Pelham. Also restyled were the long-wheelbase coupes, which got a new "gaping mouth" grille and small tailfins. **6.** Presidents continued on their longer 120.5-inch wheelbase and were offered as two- and four-door sedans with prices ranging from $2188 to $2489.

6

1

2

3

1-2. Packard donated the big 352-cubic-inch 275-horsepower V-8 that was squeezed under the long hood of the newly named Golden Hawk—the top trim level of Studebaker's long-wheelbase coupes. Ads claimed the engine gave the Golden Hawk a "hurricane of power." Other versions of the coupe continued in hardtop and pillared forms with six-cylinder or 259/289-cid V-8 power under the names Flight Hawk, Power Hawk, and Sky Hawk. **3.** The top-line Pinehurst wagon had a 289-cid V-8 and a $2529 price tag.

SCORECARD		1956
MAKE	TOTAL PRODUCTION	RANK
CLIPPER	18,482	16th
PACKARD	10,353 ▼	18th ▼
STUDEBAKER	69,593 ▼	13th ▼

1

1-3. Packards moved to a body shared with Studebaker for 1957, and were built alongside them in Studebaker's factory in South Bend, Indiana. Styling was similar, though Packards carried their signature cathedral taillights. Packard's lineup was trimmed to just the four-door Town Sedan and the four-door Country Sedan, actually a station wagon—Packard's first since 1950. They were priced at $3212 and $3384, respectively, placing the sedan between the former Clipper and Packard Executive. Furthermore, both stood about $700 north of comparable Studebakers. The only engine was a supercharged version of Studebaker's 289-cubic-inch V-8 rated at 275 horsepower. Of course, these were Packards in name only, and sales dwindled to just 3940 sedans and 869 wagons.

2

3

1

2

1. Studebaker's redesigned 1957 mainstream models weren't nearly the flop that Packard's were. Meanwhile, the long-wheelbase Loewy coupes grew tailfins, and the line was reduced to just the top V-8-only Golden Hawk hardtop coupe and six-cylinder and V-8 Silver Hawk pillared coupe. **2.** Silver Hawks started at $2142 with a six-cylinder engine, $2263 with a 289-cubic-inch V-8. That was little more than a midline Chevrolet two-door sedan, so it's odd that just 15,000 of the sporty Silver Hawks were sold. **3.** Studebaker's station wagons had previously come only in two-door form, but the '57 redesign brought four-door versions as well. The top four-door wagon was the $2666 Broadmoor. Once again, Studebakers were offered with a choice of 185-cid/101-horsepower six, or 259/289-cid V-8s with 180-225 hp.

3

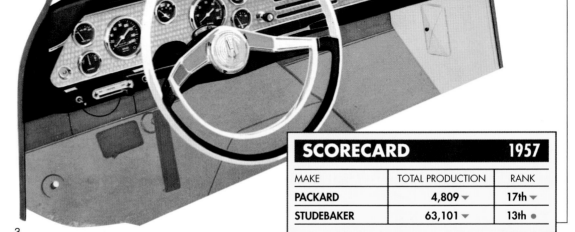

1-3. With Packard no longer building the big 352-cubic-inch 275-horsepower V-8 that so briskly propelled the Golden Hawk in 1956, Studebaker's beautiful hardtop coupe had to look elsewhere for power in '57. What it found was another Packard engine—or at least, another engine *used* in Packards. Actually, it was Studebaker's own 289-cid V-8 fitted with a Paxton supercharger, which resulted in the same 275 hp—and 100 pounds less weight. Ads claimed it provided "extra power the instant you need it." Aside from being Studebaker's only hardtop coupe, Golden Hawks could be identified by a long bulge in their hoods. Inside, round gauges set in an engine-turned dash panel befitting the car's sporty nature. Priced at $3182, only 4356 Golden Hawks were sold.

SCORECARD		1957
MAKE	TOTAL PRODUCTION	RANK
PACKARD	4,809 ▼	17th ▼
STUDEBAKER	63,101 ▼	13th ●

1

2

3

4

1. Packard tried—perhaps a bit too hard—to project a fresh face for 1958. Quad headlights (adopted by nearly all 1958 cars) and a wide-mouth grille were surrounded by housings that appeared to be tacked on, though a sloping hood with built-in scoop was an aesthetic plus. Brochures called the new look "the most original styling on the road." Indeed. Mainstream Packards lost the supercharged engine they gained in '57, using instead a nonsupercharged Studebaker 289 with 210 horsepower. **2.** Rarest of the 1958 Packards—which were pretty rare in any form—was the $3384 wagon. **3.** Added to the line was this svelte $3262 two-door hardtop, but it hardly helped sales, as just 675 were built. **4.** Also new was the Hawk hardtop coupe, which was pretty obviously just a Studebaker Golden Hawk made to look as though it was trying to swallow a frisbee. It was the only Packard to use the supercharged 289 V-8, as did the Golden Hawk. As such, the Hawk's lofty $3995 sticker—a mighty $710 more than a Golden Hawk—attracted just 588 buyers. All told, Packard sold just 2622 cars for 1958, and finally decided to throw in the towel—about two years too late.

1-3. Studebaker's 1958 restyle looked quite good—if you were far enough away not to notice the tacked-on quad headlight bezels shared with Packards. A wraparound grille was topped by a more upright hood (carried over from '57), that ads claimed "combine to impart a high-fashion elegance." Also shared with Packard was this rakish two-door hardtop body style, called the Starlight. Available in Commander (with 259-cubic-inch V-8) and top-line President trim (shown here, with 289-cid V-8), they sold for $2493 and $2695, respectively.

1

2

3

1

2

3

1. A surprising 1958 hit for Studebaker was the no-frills Scotsman, which wore the '57 front end and an amazingly modest amount of chrome—this *was* the Fifties, after all. Offered as two- and four-door sedans and a two-door wagon, they sold for $1795 to $2055, about $380 less than comparable Champions. **2.** Other mainstream Studebakers wore what ads called "Hawk-inspired body styling," and should have sold better than they did. They would prove to be the last of these larger cars Studebaker would build. **3.** Golden Hawks, still with a super-charged 289-cubic-inch V-8, sold just 878 copies for 1958. Silver Hawks did much better and would live on, but the Golden Hawk name would fly no more.

SCORECARD		1958
MAKE	TOTAL PRODUCTION	RANK
PACKARD	2,622 ▼	19th ▼
STUDEBAKER	44,759 ▼	14th ▼

1

2

1. Studebaker dropped its "regular sized" cars for 1959 and put all its money on the compact Lark. Larks were considerably shorter and lighter than their predecessors, but still offered ample interior room—as this ad strives to show. Base engine in the Lark VI was the little 169-cubic-inch six resurrected from '54, now rated at 90 horsepower. The 259-cid V-8, providing 180 to 195 hp, was standard in the Lark VIII. **2-4.** Though Larks started as low as $1925—about $250 less than the cheapest Chevy—this flashy Lark VI hardtop was a little more precious at $2275. **5.** Most expensive of the Larks was the Lark VIII two-door wagon at $2590.

3

4

5

1

1. The Loewy coupes carried on sans the hardtop Golden Hawk version for 1959. Pillared Silver Hawks were available in six-cylinder form for $2360 and with the 259-cubic-inch V-8 for $2495. Though sales would never again top 9000 units a year, the Hawk would live on almost as long as Studebaker itself. Larks, by contrast, would prove enormously popular (at least by Studebaker standards), and would keep the company aloft until the volley of compacts from other American manufacturers finally shot it down in 1966, killing Studebaker along with it.

SCORECARD		1959
MAKE	TOTAL PRODUCTION	RANK
STUDEBAKER	129,156 ▲	11th ▲